I0110746

GLOBAL GENOCIDE
of the Modern Age

First published by LAUREN MOOI Publishing

Copyright © 2025 by Dr. R. Van Reenen

All rights reserved. No part of this publication may be reproduced, stored, or transmitted in any form or by any means, electronic, mechanical, photocopying, recording, scanning, or otherwise, without written permission from the author. It is illegal to copy this book, post it to a website, or distribute it by any other means without permission.

Dr. R. Van Reenen asserts the moral right to be identified as the author of this work under the Copyright Act 98 of 1978

First Edition July 2025 in paperback

ISBN: 978-1-0370-9838-3

www.laurenmooipublishing.com

LAUREN MOOI
P U B L I S H I N G
S E R V I C E S

GLOBAL GENOCIDE
of the Modern Age

by

Dr. R Van Reenen

Table of Contents

Preface

I am deeply moved by the weight of the message contained within the pages of *"Global Genocide of the Modern Age."* This book is not just an exposé on the dangers of processed foods but a call to action, an urgent plea for us to reconsider the food choices we make every day, the systems that sustain them, and the consequences of our collective negligence. For many years, we have seen the widespread impact of modern diets on the health of individuals and communities. Obesity, diabetes, heart disease, and countless other ailments have risen dramatically, yet the root causes are often dismissed, ignored, or misunderstood. This book is an attempt to cut through the noise, to bring clarity to the conversation, and to shine a light on the devastating consequences of processed foods, not just on our physical health but also on our spiritual, mental, and emotional well-being. The title of this book, *Global Genocide of the Modern Age*, may seem strong, even provocative. But it is the only term I can use to describe the destruction that is occurring. We are witnessing the gradual decay of humanity, not just in terms of our bodies, but in the fabric of our societies. The food systems that govern our lives have been hijacked by corporate interests that prioritise profit over people, and the results have been catastrophic. More than ever, we are seeing how processed, artificial foods are poisoning our bodies, minds, and spirits. As a Christian and as a student of the Scriptures, I believe that the Bible offers profound insight into God's design for food and its purpose in our lives. We were created to flourish, to live in harmony with the earth, to care for it, and to nourish our bodies with the goodness that God has provided. Yet, the rise of processed foods has led us away from God's divine intention and into a world of convenience, excess, and destruction.

This book, however, is not just about the problem; it is about the solution. It challenges us to think beyond our appetites and to understand the far-reaching implications of our food choices. But more importantly, it calls us to action. It encourages us to step up, to become informed, and to take responsibility for the global food systems that are affecting millions of people around the world. This is not a fight that can be won by individuals alone. We must join as communities, nations, and as faithful believers who recognise the need for a restoration of what has been lost. The message of this book is ultimately one of hope. While the situation is dire, there is still time for change. The Church, our governments, and each of us as individuals have the power to make a difference. It will require sacrifice, it will require commitment, and it will require a shift in mindset. But if we are willing to embrace God's plan for health and food, we can turn the tide and create a sustainable future for generations to come.

I invite you, the reader, to approach this book with an open heart and a willing spirit. Take its words to heart, for it is not only a message for today but for the future of humanity. In the pages that follow, you will find both wisdom and conviction, a call to return to the original design that God intended for us, to restore balance, and to ensure that our choices today will bless the world tomorrow.

May you be moved to action, to reflection, and to prayer, as we all engage in this necessary journey toward the healing and restoration of the global food system.

With blessings,
Dr. R. Van Reenen

Introduction: Return to Eden

There was a time when every bite humanity took was sacred. No labels, no warnings, no chemicals, just the raw, nourishing intention of a Creator who made food not only for survival but for worship, wellness, and fellowship. That place was Eden.

In Eden, food was life. God said, *"Behold, I have given you every herb bearing seed... and every tree, in which is the fruit of a tree yielding seed; to you it shall be for meat"* (Genesis 1:29 NIV). This was not a suggestion; it was a divine prescription. A perfect, plant-based diet rich in nutrients, untouched by pollution, was handed to mankind. There were no pharmacies in Eden because food was medicine. There were no hospitals because there was no sickness. What happened?

This book is a prophetic cry and a scientific unveiling of a global genocide that is not fought with guns or bombs, but with groceries. The most effective weapon of mass destruction today is processed food, packaged in colourful boxes, marketed with smiles, and loaded with death. What began as divine sustenance has been hijacked by corporations, manipulated by chemicals, and sold back to us as convenience. It's not only killing our bodies, it's eroding our minds, sterilising our children, and desecrating our connection with God.

We are now living far from Eden. And the distance isn't just spiritual, it's dietary. This book will expose the silent war being waged against humanity and offer a pathway back, not just to health, but to holiness. You were made in God's image, not a laboratory's design. Let's return to Eden.

Chapter 1

The Original Diet
What Did God Intend?

The foundation of human health began in a garden. Before religion, before governments, before technology, there was Eden, and in it, God's perfect nutritional plan.

1.1 God's First Meal Plan

The first recorded diet in history is found in Genesis 1:29 NIV: *"And God said, Behold, I have given you every herb bearing seed... and every tree, in which is the fruit of a tree yielding seed; to you it shall be for meat."* Notice the language: "given you." It wasn't earned, farmed, or processed. It was a divine gift. The word "meat" here doesn't refer to animal flesh but to food in general, specifically, seed-bearing plants and fruits. This tells us several things:

- God intended food to be natural, plant-based, and life-giving
- The diet was designed to be both sustainable and self-replicating; every seed meant another plant

- There was no cooking, frying, canning, or processing

Adam and Eve were not given tools to manipulate food; they were given access to a fully formed, nourishing ecosystem. Everything they needed was on a branch, in the soil, or growing in plain sight. Food was not separate from their environment; it *was* their environment.

1.2 Food and Fellowship

Eating in Eden was not just a biological act; it was a spiritual one. Every meal was an act of communion with the Creator. Eating was sacred, rhythmic, and a deeply relational experience. In Eden:

- There were no food allergies
- There were no processed sugars or genetically modified organisms
- There were no deadlines, lunch breaks, or binge eating
- There was only wholeness: body, soul, and spirit in harmony

When sin entered the world, everything changed. But before we go there, we must first understand just how pure God's original design was.

1.3 The Tree of Life vs. the Tree of Knowledge

Two trees stood in the centre of Eden: The Tree of Life and the Tree of the Knowledge of Good and Evil. One gave eternal life; the other brought death. *"But of the tree of the knowledge of*

good and evil, thou shalt not eat of it..." (Genesis 2:17 NIV).
God's boundaries on diet were also boundaries on destiny.
Eating the wrong thing wasn't just a poor nutritional choice;
it was disobedience. The first sin involved food. The first
temptation was not with sex, money, or violence; it was with
a fruit. This is not accidental. Satan still uses food to tempt,
enslave, and destroy. But instead of a tree in a garden, he now
offers aisles in supermarkets. Instead of a snake's whisper, he
uses glossy commercials and false nutritional labels. And still,
mankind eats and dies.

1.4 Eden's Menu

A breakdown of the Edenic diet includes:

- Fruits – God's natural sugar, filled with antioxidants and
  vitamins
- Vegetables – Roots, leaves, and stems with minerals and
  enzymes
- Nuts and Seeds – Healthy fats, protein, and life-packed
  nutrients
- Herbs – Medicinal plants for healing and flavour

These four groups were all that Adam and Eve needed. There
was no lack, no deficiency. Everything necessary for energy,
immunity, reproduction, and brain function was included.
Compare that with today's average processed meal:

- Artificial colours
- Synthetic preservatives
- Hormone-laced meat

- High-fructose corn syrup
- GMOs, and
- Over 3,000 food additives approved for human consumption

It's not the same menu. And we are not the same people.

1.5 Health Without Hospitals

Eden had no healthcare system because the environment was the healthcare system.

- The soil was alive with minerals
- The water was unpolluted and flowing
- The air was free of industrial toxins
- The sun provided Vitamin D in perfect balance

Adam lived 930 years. Even after the Fall, the first generation lived for centuries. Methuselah lived 969 years. These were not myths; they were humans operating closer to God's original blueprint. Diet was a critical part of that longevity. The question we must ask is this: If God's diet produced life, what is today's diet producing? The next chapter will reveal the terrible consequences of abandoning the Edenic blueprint, and how the first bite outside the garden began a food curse we are still paying for.

Chapter 2

The Fall and the Food Curse

The moment Adam and Eve took that forbidden bite, everything changed. The sweetness of the fruit turned bitter in the mouth of humanity. What began as a perfect, divinely ordered nutritional system collapsed into a struggle for survival. Food, which was once freely provided in abundance, became a source of pain, effort, decay, and ultimately, death.

2.1 The Bite That Broke the World

Genesis 3:6 NIV tells us: *"And when the woman saw that the tree was good for food... she took of the fruit thereof, and did eat, and gave also unto her husband with her; and he did eat."* This was the moment that humanity's physical and spiritual diet changed forever. It was not only disobedience; it was an inversion of divine order. Adam and Eve ate something that looked good, not something that was commanded. They chose perception over instruction, appetite over alignment. And just as the wrong food choice corrupted the soul, so too it corrupted the soil.

2.2 Cursed Ground, Corrupted Growth

Immediately after the fall, God did not curse humanity directly with disease, but He did curse the ground: *"Cursed is the ground for thy sake; in sorrow shalt thou eat of it all the days of thy life; Thorns also and thistles shall it bring forth to thee; and thou shalt eat the herb of the field; In the sweat of thy face shalt thou eat bread..."* (Genesis 3:17–19 NIV). Let that sink in. The very ground that once effortlessly produced food now resisted man. The environment became hostile. The earth, once our servant, became our rival.

- Thorns and thistles symbolise not just weeds, but toxic, mutated growth
- Sweat and sorrow replaced abundance and ease
- Bread, once symbolic of life, now came from toil and brokenness

The Fall birthed the first famine, not of food, but of purity. Food now had to be worked for, processed, and protected from decay.

2.3 From Garden to Grave

After being expelled from Eden, Adam and Eve no longer had access to the Tree of Life. This is key. In Eden, food was linked to eternal life. Outside Eden, food was linked to mortality. *"...lest he put forth his hand, and take also of the tree of life, and eat, and live forever..."* (Genesis 3:22 NIV). God removed access to life-giving food to prevent eternal life in a fallen state. This act was merciful, but it also meant that humanity would now experience degeneration, aging, and decay.

Thus, began humanity's descent into:

- Rotting food, requiring salt, smoke, or fermentation to preserve
- Spoilage, leading to hunger and famine
- Agricultural struggle, with droughts, floods, and disease

In short, our diet died with Eden. And the funeral was global.

2.4 The Introduction of Animal Consumption

The first recorded death in Scripture was not a murder; it was a sacrifice for clothing. God made garments for Adam and Eve from animal skins (Genesis 3:21 NIV), hinting at the future use of animals in both survival and atonement. But it wasn't until after the flood that meat entered the human diet: *"Every moving thing that lived shall be meat for you; even as the green herb have, I given you all things."* (Genesis 9:3 NIV). Why the shift? Several reasons are debated:

- The earth post-flood may have lacked fertile vegetation
- Man's life was already shortened by sin
- Sacrificial systems required animal familiarity

But this shift came with a consequence. Life spans began to plummet:

- Adam: 930 years
- Noah: 950 years

- Shem: 600 years
- Abraham: 175 years
- Moses: 120 years

By the time of King David, the average lifespan was 70–80 years (Psalm 90:10 NIV). Something had dramatically changed, and meat consumption was part of that story.

2.5 From Sacrifice to Slaughterhouse

What began as an occasional necessity became a habitual indulgence. Over time:

- Animal fat became a delicacy
- Blood consumption (forbidden in Leviticus 17:10–12 NIV) became common in pagan cultures
- Idol worship merged with meat feasts

Even in Israel, God placed strict limits:

- No unclean animals
- No fat or blood
- Slaughter had to be purposeful and sacred

Today, however, meat is no longer a sacred gift; it's a processed, hormone-injected, factory-produced product, often consumed three times a day. We have turned the altar of sacrifice into a conveyor belt of death.

2.6 The Psychological Shift

Post-Eden, food became linked to fear, survival, and indulgence. This psychological shift altered the human relationship with eating:

- Scarcity bred hoarding
- Guilt bred gluttony
- Shame bred secrecy

This is evident in the wilderness generation. Though God provided manna from heaven (Exodus 16 NIV), the Israelites craved meat, crying out for Egypt's menu instead of God's miracle. In response, God sent quail, and a plague followed (Numbers 11 NIV). Why? Because rejecting God's food is rejecting God's authority.

2.7 Today's Curse Continues

The curse on food has only worsened:

- The soil is depleted by over-farming and pesticides
- Seeds are genetically modified
- Water sources are polluted
- Animals are factory farmed with antibiotics and growth hormones
- Crops are sprayed with chemicals linked to cancer and infertility

In essence, modern food systems are built not on God's design, but man's defiance. We have recreated Babel on our plates, technological arrogance at the cost of divine obedience.

2.8 Prophetic Pattern: From Eden to Babylon

Every time humanity moves away from God, food becomes distorted.

- In Egypt, Joseph had to store grain to prevent famine.
- In Babylon, Daniel had to refuse the king's food to stay pure (Daniel 1 NIV).
- In Revelation, economic control is exerted through buying and selling, and even food is weaponised.

This is not just history; it is prophecy unfolding. The global food system is becoming a beast system, controlling who lives, who eats, and who survives.

Final Reflection: What Are We Eating Today?

Ask yourself:

- Is this what God gave in Eden?
- Or is this the product of fallen soil and cursed systems?
- Am I eating what gives life, or what steals it?

The fall broke more than man's innocence; it broke the food chain. But there is hope. The next chapter will trace the survival of God's dietary laws through the ages and how some still chose obedience over indulgence.

Chapter 3

Biblical Nutrition Through the Ages

Though Eden was lost, God did not leave humanity without guidance. Across generations, through patriarchs, prophets, and even plagues, the Creator consistently provided *nutritional instructions*, laws, habits, and principles that preserved both physical health and spiritual alignment. In this chapter, we explore how God's design for food was not erased after Eden; it was *revealed afresh* through the Scriptures, tested in crises, and preserved among the obedient.

3.1 Noah and the Post-Flood Diet

After the flood, the earth was wiped clean, but the soil had changed. Vegetation was not immediately abundant, so God made an exception for meat: *"Every moving thing that lives shall be food for you. And as I gave you the green plants, I give you everything."* – Genesis 9:3 NIV. However, this permission came with a warning: *"But you shall not eat flesh with its life, that is, its blood."* – Genesis 9:4 NIV. This distinction is critical. God introduced boundaries, a recognition that even if meat was allowed, not all parts of it were meant for consumption. This was not permission to devour indiscriminately. It was a temporary provision. A fallback, not a feast.

3.2 Abraham: Simplicity and Sacred Feasts

Abraham, the father of faith, lived in a culture surrounded by idolatrous and indulgent food practices. But his life was marked by:

- Simplicity in meals (Genesis 18:6–8 NIV)
- Hospitality with moderation
- And offerings that honoured God

His diet, though not extensively documented, reflected natural, home-prepared, locally-sourced foods, and importantly, occasional meat, not daily indulgence. He offered bread, milk, and a calf to the three angelic visitors, symbolising balance between grains, dairy, and meat, in that order. Today's diet reverses this completely; we lead with meat, follow with sugar, and forget the bread of life.

3.3 Moses and the Levitical Food Laws

Nowhere is God's nutritional system more explicit than in the Law of Moses. In Leviticus 11 and Deuteronomy 14, God outlines clean vs. unclean animals. The laws are clear, practical, and often echoed by modern science:

Clean Animals;

- Land: Animals that chew the cud and have split hooves (e.g., cows, sheep)
- Water: Fish with fins and scales
- Birds: Certain fowl, like chickens and doves

Unclean Animals;
- Pigs, camels, rabbits
- Shellfish, eels, and catfish
- Raptors, scavenger birds
- Reptiles and insects (except locusts)

God didn't forbid certain foods for ritualistic reasons alone. Many unclean animals are scavengers; nature's garbage collectors. Eating them is like consuming a sponge full of toxins. *"For I am the LORD your God. Consecrate yourselves therefore, and be holy... You shall not defile yourselves with any swarming thing..."* – Leviticus 11:44 NIV. These laws were not abolished by Christ (Matthew 5:17 NIV) but fulfilled in meaning. They still carry wisdom for those who heed God's voice.

3.4 Manna: Divine Superfood in the Wilderness

God miraculously fed His people in the wilderness with manna, a substance unlike anything before or since. "It was like coriander seed, white, and the taste of it was like wafers made with honey." – Exodus 16:31 NIV. Manna was:

- Plant-based
- Lightweight
- Spoil-resistant (for one day)

- Complete in nutrition (sustained millions for 40 years)

Yet the Israelites grew tired of it and lusted after meat. God gave them quail and sent a plague as judgment (Numbers 11:31–33 NIV). This teaches us a sobering truth: God's ideal diet is often rejected in favour of our cravings. But rejecting divine nutrition comes at a deadly cost.

3.5 Daniel's Diet: A Rebellion of Righteousness

In Babylon, Daniel and his friends were offered royal food: rich meats, wine, and delicacies. Yet Daniel refused, choosing instead: *"Give us vegetables to eat and water to drink."* – Daniel 1:12 NIV. After ten days, Daniel and his friends were:

- Healthier
- Stronger
- More mentally alert

This was not just a fast; it was a protest against Babylon's system. Daniel's diet was a declaration: *"I will not be nourished by the empire that enslaves me."* This principle echoes today. Choosing God's food is an act of spiritual resistance against a processed world.

3.6 Jesus: Bread, Fish, and the Final Feast

Jesus frequently used food in ministry:

- Multiplying loaves and fish (natural, not farmed)
- Teaching with images of grains, seeds, and vines

- Breaking unleavened bread at Passover

His diet would have been consistent with Jewish purity laws, clean meats, olive oil, figs, lentils, and herbs. He never promoted indulgence. He fasted for 40 days, a practice that modern medicine is rediscovering as profoundly healing. Jesus called Himself the "Bread of Life," not the "Meat of Life" or "Wine of Life." In Him, the divine food code culminated in spiritual nourishment.

3.7 Revelation and the Tree of Life Restored

The story of biblical nutrition ends where it began, in Edenic restoration. *"To the one who conquers... I will grant you to eat of the tree of life, which is in the paradise of God."* – Revelation 2:7 NIV. And again, in Revelation 22: *"On either side of the river, was the tree of life... and the leaves of the tree were for the healing of the nations."* This is not an allegory alone. God is declaring that His food, pure, plant-based, and life-giving, will return to humanity. Not through science, but through sanctification.

Final Reflection: Why Biblical Food Matters Today

Modern nutrition systems ignore biblical wisdom. We:

- Reject clean/unclean distinctions
- Indulge in sugar, additives, and artificial foods
- Prioritise quantity over purity

But God's design is timeless.

What if the biblical diet is not outdated, but divinely protective? What if our health crises are less about genetics and more about *disobedience*? In the next chapter, we'll examine how processed food became the enemy, how corporations, chemicals, and convenience hijacked our tables, and how what we eat today would be unrecognisable in Eden or even ancient Israel.

Chapter 4

The Rise of Processed Food
From Shelf to Sickness

Humanity has moved far from Eden's gardens and Daniel's pulses. In less than a century, the global diet has undergone a radical transformation, from *fresh and local* to *boxed and chemical*. What sits on our shelves today is not food in the biblical or biological sense. It is an *engineered substance*, designed for profit, not for nourishment. This chapter exposes how processed food became the new global diet, the deadly shift from natural to artificial, and how this transformation is systematically destroying the human race.

4.1 The Industrial Revolution of Food

The dawn of the 20th century brought with it machines, factories, and efficiency. But it also brought the death of the family farm. With urbanisation came a demand for:

- Shelf-stable goods
- Fast preparation

- Mass distribution

Thus, food industrialisation began:

- Canning and bottling
- Pasteurisation and irradiation
- Freezing and microwaving

Food was no longer something grown; it was something *manufactured*. With speed and shelf life came loss of nutrition and rise of additives.

4.2 The Invasion of Additives and Preservatives

To make food last longer, look better, and taste more addictive, manufacturers introduced:

- Preservatives (sodium benzoate, nitrates)
- Colourants (Red 40, Yellow 5)
- Artificial flavours (MSG, esters)
- Sweeteners (aspartame, sucralose)
- Texture agents (gums, emulsifiers)

Most of these chemicals:

- Do not exist in nature
- Cannot be digested properly
- Are linked to cancer, ADHD, infertility, and metabolic disorders

Processed food does not decay quickly. Why? Because *it is too toxic for even bacteria to consume.* If fungi won't touch it, why should you?

4.3 Sugar: The Silent Killer

Perhaps no substance has been weaponised more than refined sugar. Once rare and expensive, it is now everywhere:

- Sodas
- Sauces
- Breads
- Breakfast cereals

Sugar is:

- More addictive than cocaine (confirmed by multiple studies)
- A leading cause of type 2 diabetes, obesity, and heart disease
- A fuel for cancer cell proliferation

The average child today consumes over 20 teaspoons of sugar per day, more than ten times what the body can handle. This is not nutrition. It is *poison marketed as pleasure.*

4.4 GMO and Synthetic Food: Playing God with Genes

Genetically Modified Organisms (GMOs) were introduced under the guise of food security. But beneath the surface lies a darker truth:

- Crops altered to resist herbicides like glyphosate (Roundup)
- Patented seeds owned by corporate giants like Monsanto
- Plants grown in labs, stripped of biodiversity

Genetic tampering has led to:

- Allergic reactions
- Hormonal imbalances
- Soil degradation
- Loss of natural seed heritage

God never created corn that produces its own pesticide. This is not agriculture; it is genetic warfare.

4.5 Fast Food Nation: Speed Over Safety

Fast food is the crown jewel of processed food culture. With drive-throughs and dollar menus, we traded:

- Time for taste
- Quality for convenience
- Health for hurry

Most fast food contains:

- Hydrogenated oils (trans fats)
- High-fructose corn syrup
- Artificial meat flavouring
- Plastic-based packaging that leaks into food

And yet, these chains are global empires. McDonald's feeds about 1% of the world's population daily. What would Jesus say about a generation that feasts at Golden Arches while ignoring His table?

4.6 Big Food, Big Lies: The Corporate Control of Diet

Behind every colourful cereal box, seductive commercial, and "low-fat" label lies a profit-driven system:

- Lobbyists influence food policy
- Advertisers target children
- "Healthy" labels mask toxic ingredients
- Scientific studies are funded by the very companies they claim to assess

Companies like Nestlé, PepsiCo, Unilever, and Coca-Cola control most of the food and beverage brands worldwide. Their goal is not your health; it is your habitual consumption. We are not eating food. We are eating marketing.

4.7 The Cost: A Sick and Dying Generation

Processed food has given us:

- A rise in childhood obesity and early-onset diabetes
- Infertility and hormonal disorders in men and women
- Cancer linked to nitrates, BPA, and acrylamide
- Neurological damage from food dyes and artificial sweeteners

Our hospitals are overflowing, not because of viruses, but because of diets. We are malnourished in a world of overabundance. What Eden gave us in fruit and grain; Babylon now offers in burgers and chips.

Final Reflection: Eden on Trial

If Adam were alive today and placed in a modern supermarket, what would he say? Would he recognise the sugary drinks, boxed dinners, and neon candies as food? Or would he weep, seeing the image of God desecrated by artificial consumption? This is not progress. This is perversion. We must return. Not to caveman diets or fad detoxes, but to *Edenic wisdom*. To food that heals, not harms. To nutrition that honours the Creator. In the next chapter, we'll expose the global food conspiracy; how governments, corporations, and media intentionally manipulate what you eat, and why your destruction is *not accidental*, but *engineered.*

Chapter 5

The Global Food Conspiracy
Who Profits from Our Poison?

Humans are being slowly exterminated, not by warheads or bullets, but by what lies on our plates. This is not a random epidemic. It is an organised assault, a conspiracy that flows from boardrooms, governments, and global media into the bloodstream of nations. The question is not *"How did this happen?"* but rather *"Who made it happen, and why?"* This chapter unearths the hidden hands behind the processed food empire, exposing how greed, control, and manipulation are fuelling the genocide of the modern age.

5.1 Follow the Money: The Corporations Behind the Curtain

The world's food is controlled by a handful of conglomerates. These companies operate behind countless brands, labels, and logos, but they are all rooted in the same corporate soil:

- Nestlé – over 2,000 brands in over 190 countries

- PepsiCo – owners of Frito-Lay, Quaker, Tropicana, and Gatorade
- Unilever – controls more than 400 brands, including food and hygiene products
- Kraft Heinz – one of the world's largest processed food giants
- Coca-Cola – more than 200 brands across beverages and snacks

These corporations are not committed to your health. Their business thrives on:

- Cheap ingredients
- Addictive flavours
- Low production costs
- High profit margins

They are not selling food. They are selling illness in digestible packaging.

5.2 Government Complicity: Silent Allies in Power

You would expect governments to protect public health. Instead, they collaborate with poisoners:

- Subsidising crops like corn and soy, which are turned into unhealthy oils and syrups
- Allowing harmful additives banned in Europe to remain legal in countries like the U.S., South Africa, and Brazil
- Accepting billions in lobbying funds from food corporations to influence policy

- Silencing independent food scientists and whistleblowers

Regulators like the FDA, EFSA, and FAO often act not as defenders of people but as gatekeepers for industry. The prophet Isaiah's warning comes alive again: *"Woe to those who call evil good, and good evil..."* (Isaiah 5:20 NIV).

5.3 Marketing Deception: Feeding Lies to the Masses

The battlefield is no longer the farm; it's the mind. Marketing has become a weapon of mass manipulation:

- "Low-fat" products overloaded with sugar
- "Healthy" cereals with 40% added sweeteners
- Bright packaging with cartoon characters to seduce children
- Celebrity endorsements by athletes for junk drinks
- "Natural" labels with zero regulation behind the term

The processed food industry uses psychological warfare:

- Colours that trigger appetite
- Scents pumped into supermarkets
- Background music to make you linger longer

They are not just selling food; they are programming behaviour.

5.4 The Media Collusion: Silence, Sponsorship, and Smoke Screens

Why don't you see exposés about these dangers on the news? Why do food documentaries disappear from platforms? Because mainstream media is funded by the same companies that profit from disease.

- Ad revenue from junk food companies keeps TV stations silent
- Social media influencers are paid to promote products disguised as "reviews."
- "Health" magazines recommend toxic foods in exchange for sponsorship

Even children's shows and cartoons now feature subtle product placements for candy, soda, and fast food. The media isn't failing us. It's *betraying* us.

5.5 Pharmaceutical Companies: The Back-End Profiteers

Here is the most wicked part of the conspiracy: The same companies making you sick are tied to the companies selling the cure.

- Obesity leads to diabetes → Insulin sales skyrocket
- Processed food causes cancer → Chemotherapy markets boom
- Sugar triggers inflammation → Statin and anti-inflammatory drug use increases

The food industry and Big Pharma are two wings of the same vulture, circling over humanity's health for profit. A healthy population is unprofitable. A chronically sick, dependent population? That's *gold*.

5.6 Population Control and Eugenics: A Darker Agenda?

Is it just about profit? Or is there a deeper, more sinister plan? History shows us that empires have always tried to:

- Control population growth
- Manipulate the weak
- Eliminate the poor and the undesirable

From Nazi eugenics to Planned Parenthood's racist roots, the idea of selective survival is not new.
Could processed food be the soft genocide of the 21st century?

- It disables reproductive health
- It shortens lifespans
- It increases mental illness
- It targets poor communities with the cheapest, deadliest options

This is no longer just about food. It is about who lives, who dies, and who decides.

Final Reflection: God's Warning Ignored

In Eden, food was pure, simple, and sacred. In Babylon, food is corrupted, confusing, and cursed. *"They will eat but not be satisfied... because they have deserted the Lord."* — Hosea 4:10

NIV. We are perishing not just because of what we eat, but because we have trusted Caesar instead of Christ. We must return to the Shepherd's table, to food that comes without lies, additives, or agendas.

In the next chapter, we dive into The Health Fallout — How Processed Food Is Destroying the Human Body. We will break down the physical, mental, and reproductive consequences of modern diets, with scientific studies and biblical parallels.

Chapter 6

The Health Fallout
How Processed Food Is Destroying the Human Body

Every bite we take carries a consequence. In Eden, food brought life. In today's processed world, food brings decay, disease, and death. The human body, created in God's image to thrive on natural sustenance, is now collapsing under the weight of chemically engineered "foods" designed for shelves, not stomachs. This chapter unpacks the devastating impact of processed food on the human body, from head to toe. We will explore its destruction of physical health, mental clarity, hormonal balance, fertility, and long-term vitality.

6.1 The Human Temple: Designed for Eden

"Do you not know that your bodies are temples of the Holy Spirit...?" — 1 Corinthians 6:19 NIV. God's design for the human body was perfect. Every cell, organ, and system were built to work in harmony, fed by clean water, fresh plants, and pure meat. Eden was not only a spiritual sanctuary; it was a

nutritional blueprint. Modern diets ignore this blueprint. Instead of organic life, we feed our temples:

- Chemically dyed food
- Sugary toxins
- Genetically modified organisms
- Hormone-disrupting packaging

The result? A worldwide health crisis; engineered, preventable, and entirely man-made.

6.2 Digestive Disaster: Gut Health Under Attack

The gut is often called the "second brain." It is the core of the immune system and central to nutrient absorption. Processed foods:

- Strip the gut of beneficial bacteria
- Introduce harmful emulsifiers and preservatives
- Weaken the intestinal lining, causing leaky gut syndrome
- Promote chronic bloating, gas, ulcers, and IBS

The Bible describes clean and unclean foods, not only spiritually, but for bodily wholeness. When we ignore these principles, we destroy the digestive engine God designed.

6.3 Obesity and Metabolic Breakdown

Modern humans are overfed but undernourished.

- Sugary drinks, processed snacks, and refined carbs overload the pancreas
- Insulin resistance develops
- Obesity becomes widespread
- Type 2 diabetes becomes a global norm

In Eden, food *sustained* life. Today's food *clogs* it. Childhood obesity has tripled in the last 30 years. Teenagers now face adult diseases. And adults die younger than their ancestors. *"Their god is their stomach..."* — Philippians 3:19 NIV. Has our appetite replaced our worship?

6.4 The Silent Epidemic: Inflammation and Autoimmune Disease

One of the most insidious effects of processed food is chronic inflammation. Additives like:

- Artificial sweeteners
- Vegetable oils (soy, canola, corn)
- Food dyes (especially Red 40, Yellow 6)
- Preservatives (nitrates, BHA, BHT)

...trigger the body's immune system into overdrive. This constant state of alert leads to:

- Arthritis
- Lupus
- Fibromyalgia
- Crohn's disease
- Psoriasis

The immune system begins attacking the body itself because the body is constantly ingesting foreign invaders disguised as food.

6.5 Cancer: Fuelling the Fire of Mutation

Cancer is not random. In many cases, it is dietary. Carcinogenic compounds are rampant in:

- Burned meats
- Artificial sweeteners
- Processed meats (bacon, sausage)
- Plastic packaging (BPA)
- Microwave meals (acrylamide)

The World Health Organisation classifies processed meats as Group 1 carcinogens, the same level as asbestos and tobacco. Yet they are still advertised to children. Cancer is not only a disease. It is a symptom of a poisoned generation.

6.6 Hormonal Chaos: The Endocrine System Hijacked

Processed foods destroy hormonal balance:

- Soy-based products mimic oestrogen
- Plastic containers leach hormone disruptors
- Dairy and meat are pumped with synthetic growth hormones

The result:

- Boys with low testosterone
- Girls with early puberty
- Infertility in both men and women
- Miscarriages and declining birth rates

This is not just a health breakdown. It is human sabotage.

6.7 Mental Decline: Fog, Depression, and Neurodegeneration

The brain is under siege. Processed food affects:

- Serotonin production (90% of which is made in the gut)
- Neuroplasticity and learning
- Emotional regulation and mood stability

Links have been found between poor diets and:

- Depression
- Anxiety
- ADHD
- Alzheimer's disease

Sugar-laden breakfasts and dyed snack bars are producing emotionally unstable, attention-deficient children and sedated, medicated adults. Where once manna from heaven sharpened the mind, now fake food dulls it.

Final Reflection: From Healing to Hurting

God gave food as healing: *"The fruit thereof shall be for meat, and the leaf thereof for medicine."* — Ezekiel 47:12 NIV. But man has reversed this gift. Now, food is our enemy. It no longer heals; it harms. We are dying not from starvation, but from consumption. Our diseases are not mysterious. They are manufactured.

Chapter 7

Biblical Food Laws
God's Forgotten Prescription for Health

When God created man, He also created a divine menu, not one driven by profit, preservatives, or palate addiction, but one rooted in life, holiness, and health. The Bible doesn't just offer spiritual wisdom; it outlines clear dietary laws given not as burdens but as blessings. Today, these laws are dismissed as outdated or merely cultural. But what if they were God's built-in defence system against the very diseases we now face in epidemic proportions? In this chapter, we rediscover God's nutritional instructions, grounded in the Garden of Eden and echoed through the Mosaic Law, and we ask: *What if the Bible had it right all along?*

7.1 Eden: The Original Diet of Man

"And God said, Behold, I have given you every herb bearing seed... and every tree... to you it shall be for meat." — Genesis 1:29 NIV. Before sin, before slaughter, before preservatives and plastic wrappers, there was plant-based provision:

- Fresh fruits and vegetables
- Seeds and nuts
- Naturally growing herbs
- Unpolluted water from rivers

This was God's ideal diet: living food from living soil. It wasn't until after the Fall and the Flood (Genesis 9:3 NIV) that God permitted the eating of meat, and even then, it came with conditions and restrictions.

7.2 Clean vs. Unclean: God's Health Filter

Leviticus 11 and Deuteronomy 14 outline specific animals humans are permitted to eat, those considered clean, and those they should not touch, unclean. Clean Animals:

- Land: Animals that chew the cud and have split hooves (e.g., cattle, sheep, goats)
- Water: Fish with fins and scales
- Birds: Non-scavenger birds like chicken, dove, and quail

Unclean Animals:

- Pigs (do not chew cud)
- Shellfish (no fins or scales)
- Bottom-feeders (crabs, catfish, lobsters)
- Birds of prey (eagles, vultures)
- Rodents and reptiles

These laws were not random. They were God's health protocols, long before science confirmed:

- Pork hosts parasites and viruses like trichinosis
- Shellfish accumulate toxins from polluted waters
- Scavenger birds are at high risk of zoonotic disease transmission

Modern diseases like swine flu and seafood poisoning are biblical validations.

7.3 The Kosher Principle: Clean Handling, Sacred Living

Kosher is more than tradition; it represents:

- Humane slaughter
- Removal of blood (Leviticus 17:10–14 NIV)
- Separation of meat and dairy for digestion
- Avoidance of cross-contamination

Even Jesus respected food purity: *"He did eat with them, yet sinned not..."* — Luke 24:43 (paraphrased). The early church often shared clean, simple meals, reflecting respect for the Temple of the Body.

7.4 The Role of Fasting and Feasting

God not only tells us *what* to eat, but *when* and *how*.

- Fasting resets the body, improves immune function, and restores clarity (see Daniel 1)
- Feasting was seasonal, spiritual, and mindful, not daily gluttony

"When you fast, do not look somber... but wash your face..." — Matthew 6:16-17 NIV. Modern food systems teach constant indulgence. God taught restraint, celebration, and purpose.

7.5 Biblical Healing Through Natural Remedies

Scripture also prescribes natural medicine:

- Honey: Healing for wounds and digestion (Proverbs 24:13)
- Olive oil: Anti-inflammatory, used in anointing and cooking (James 5:14)
- Figs and herbs: Used for treating disease (Isaiah 38:21)

Contrast this with today's laboratory-made food "solutions" that cause more harm than healing.

7.6 Jesus and Food: What Did the Messiah Eat?

Jesus's diet reflected simplicity, purity, and spiritual significance:

- Bread (unleavened at Passover)
- Fish (clean species, likely tilapia)
- Olives and figs
- Lamb at Passover (clean meat)

He never endorsed gluttony, processed indulgence, or food idolatry. Instead, He modelled gratitude and *mindful consumption*: *"Man shall not live by bread alone, but by every word..."* — Matthew 4:4 NIV. Even when miraculously feeding the multitudes, He multiplied natural food, not synthetic snacks.

Final Reflection: Return to Eden

Rejecting biblical food laws has led to:

- Degenerate health
- Degenerative diseases
- Generational weakness

God's Word is not only for the soul; it is nourishment for the body. The path forward is not in biotech labs or fast-food innovation, but in returning to Eden's table.

Chapter 8

The Eden Blueprint vs. the Babylonian Buffet
A Tale of Two Tables

Humanity now sits between two spiritual tables: one set by God in Eden, the other by Babylon in rebellion. What we eat is no longer a matter of taste alone; it is a matter of allegiance. In Eden, food was life-giving, healing, clean, and purposeful. In Babylon, food is addictive, profit-driven, defiled, and destructive. This chapter uncovers the battle between these two worldviews and how our daily food choices are forming our bodies, minds, and spirits, either in alignment with Heaven or assimilation into a fallen world system.

8.1 Eden's Table: The Divine Standard

The Garden of Eden provided a diet of:

- Unprocessed plant life
- Clean water from rivers
- Natural rhythms of harvest and rest

No additives. No preservatives. No manipulation. God was the Provider. Man was the steward. *"The Lord God took the man and put him in the garden... to work it and take care of it."* — Genesis 2:15 NIV. Eden's table was sacred, a space of communion, not consumerism.

8.2 Babylon's Table: The System of Control

In Scripture, Babylon symbolises confusion, rebellion, excess, and oppression. *"Babylon the Great, the mother of prostitutes and of the abominations of the earth..."* — Revelation 17:5 NIV. Its food system reflects its spirit:

- Mass production
- Genetic modification
- Food engineered for addiction
- Global monopolies profiting off sickness

In Babylon, food is no longer worship; it's weaponised.

8.3 Daniel's Stand: Choosing the Eden Diet in Babylon

One of the clearest contrasts is found in the Book of Daniel. Captive in Babylon, Daniel is offered the king's food, rich, luxurious, but unclean. *"But Daniel resolved not to defile himself with the royal food and wine..."* — Daniel 1:8 NIV.

Instead, he chooses vegetables and water. The result?

- Superior health

- Greater wisdom
- Divine favour

This ancient stand is a prophetic picture: Eden's diet preserved Daniel in a Babylonian world.

8.4 The Modern Babylonian Buffet

Today's Babylonian buffet includes:

- GMOs
- High-fructose corn syrup
- Synthetic sweeteners
- Hormone-injected meats
- Food dyes and preservatives
- Microplastics and packaging chemicals

It seduces with convenience and flavour, but delivers:

- Disease
- Mental fog
- Spiritual dullness
- Dependence on pharmaceutical "salvation."

Every aisle of the modern supermarket is a false temple with idols of artificial life.

8.5 Fast Food, Slow Death

Fast food is the epitome of Babylon's table:

- Immediate gratification
- Zero nourishment
- High addiction potential

Millions of people line up daily for meals that shorten their lifespan and fog their discernment. And tragically, this food system is marketed to the poor, making poverty a health sentence.

8.6 Churches at the Wrong Table

Even in many churches, potlucks are filled with processed foods, sugary snacks, and artificial drinks. The sacredness of food has been lost. How can we preach healing, but feed poison? How can we lay hands for deliverance, yet ignore dietary bondage? God's table brings covenant, clarity, and community. Babylon's buffet brings confusion, compromise, and corruption.

8.7 Rebuilding Eden in a Babylonian World

The call is not to escape the world but to resist its table. We can:

- Grow gardens again
- Choose whole foods
- Practice Sabbath meals with purpose
- Teach children to cook, plant, and discern
- Read food labels with the same care we read Scripture

The Eden Blueprint is still available, but it must be rebuilt one home, one meal, and one conviction at a time.

Final Reflection: Table Theology

God is always inviting us to His table: *"You prepare a table before me in the presence of my enemies..."* — Psalm 23:5 NIV. The enemy also prepares a table, but it is a trap masked as pleasure. Every bite is a spiritual decision. The question isn't *just* "What's on your plate?" The deeper question is: Whose table are you eating from?

Chapter 9

The Food Industry
Profits, Politics, and Population Control

Behind the shiny wrappers, seductive ads, and promises of "convenience" lies an uncomfortable truth: the global food industry has become one of the most powerful tools of manipulation in human history. Food is no longer cultivated with care but manufactured for control. And the modern food system is no longer about feeding people, it's about feeding profits, steering policies, and shaping populations. This chapter pulls back the corporate curtain to expose how a handful of multinational food conglomerates have hijacked health, influenced governments, and silently orchestrated a slow genocide under the guise of nourishment.

9.1 The Rise of Food Corporations

Just a few multinational corporations control most of the food you find in a grocery store. Examples include:

- Nestlé

- PepsiCo
- Unilever
- Kellogg's
- Tyson Foods
- Cargill
- Monsanto (now part of Bayer)

Each of these companies:

- Owns dozens to hundreds of brands
- Manufacturers processed, packaged, and ultra-processed foods
- Controls food from seed to shelf, leaving little room for natural variation or local farming

These corporations have shifted the world from:

- Farm to table, to
- Factory to consumer

9.2 Profit Over People

Modern food is designed not to nourish, but to:

- Addict through sugar, salt, and fat
- Preserve shelf-life, not human life
- Drive repeat purchases, not long-term health

Addictive formulas are *scientifically engineered* to hit the brain's pleasure centres, like narcotics. And the result is predictable:

- Overconsumption
- Chronic disease
- Emotional and spiritual numbness

Meanwhile, sickness creates a lucrative downstream market for:

- Pharmaceutical companies
- Medical institutions
- Health insurance firms

One system creates the disease; the other sells the cure.

9.3 Government Complicity and Regulatory Capture

Governments often appear to regulate food for public safety. But the truth is that lobbyists and corporate donations control policy.

- The FDA and USDA in America
- The EFSA in Europe
- And food regulatory boards in Africa and Asia

All have deep financial and political ties to the very corporations they are meant to oversee. Policies often allow:

- Cancer-linked preservatives
- Artificial dyes are banned in other countries
- Genetically modified organisms (GMOs) without labelling
- Pesticides like glyphosate are still in use despite global protests

Your food is being regulated by those who profit from your illness.

9.4 GMO: Genetic Manipulation and Patent Control

Genetically modified organisms (GMOs) are hailed as miracles of modern agriculture, but they come with sinister side effects:

- Patented seeds make farmers legally dependent on corporations
- Crops are modified to resist herbicides, not improve nutrition
- Long-term health impacts are still emerging cancer, allergies, and infertility

In essence, control of the seed = control of the future. *"And God said, let the earth bring forth grass... the herb yielding seed..."* — Genesis 1:11 NIV. But Babylon says, "Patent it. Sell it. Control it."

9.5 The Poor Are the First to Suffer

In low-income communities:

- The cheapest food is the most toxic
- Fast food chains saturate neighbourhoods
- Nutrition education is non-existent

The result? An epidemic of:

- Obesity
- Diabetes
- Malnutrition despite full bellies

Poverty is no longer defined by lack of food, but by lack of real food. This isn't accidental; it's an engineered dependency.

9.6 Population Control in Disguise

Throughout history, food has been a tool of domination:

- Empires starved rebels into submission
- Colonisers rewrote indigenous food systems
- Totalitarian regimes rationed food to maintain power

Today, the same tactics have been digitised and globalised:

- Food crises can be manufactured through supply chain disruptions
- Inflation can make healthy food inaccessible
- Lab-grown meat, insect protein, and food passports are emerging as the next phase of population tracking and modification

Under the guise of climate change, governments are being pressured to shift the food supply toward artificial, programmable substances.

9.7 The Role of the Church and the Watchmen

Where is the voice of the Church in this? Where are the modern-day Daniels, Josephs, and Nehemiah sounding the alarm? Too many pulpits are silent while Babylon feeds the flock poison. As shepherds, pastors, parents, and leaders, we must:

- Teach food discernment from Scripture
- Build community gardens and food banks
- Refuse partnerships with exploitative corporations
- Advocate for a policy rooted in biblical stewardship

This is a spiritual battle, not just a physical one.

Final Reflection: Who's at the Table of Your Mind?

We are not just what we eat, we are what we submit to. The food industry is not neutral. It is a throne from which Babylon exerts silent dominion. But we have a choice. God still offers the Eden blueprint. And those who dare to reject Babylon's buffet will become the remnant, healthy in body, sharp in mind, bold in spirit.

Chapter 10
The Science of Death
How Processed Foods Destroy Body, Mind, and Spirit

While many are aware of the physical consequences of processed foods, the deeper, more insidious effects reach into our emotions, thought patterns, and spiritual lives. The evidence is in: processed foods are not only altering our DNA and gut microbiota but are quietly feeding a global epidemic of chronic disease, mental disorders, and spiritual blindness. In this chapter, we will break down the scientific evidence and biological mechanisms behind how processed foods contribute to:

- Cancer
- Infertility
- Mental illness
- Spiritual numbness

10.1 What Are Processed Foods?

Processed foods are those that have undergone various treatments to alter their natural state. These processes include:

- Canning
- Freezing
- Dehydrating
- Grinding, and
- Chemical preservatives

These foods often contain:

- Artificial flavours
- Colorants
- Excessive sugars
- Refined oils
- Chemical additives, and
- GMOs

The more a food is processed, the further it moves from its natural, life-giving form.

10.2 The DNA Damage: How Chemicals Alter Our Genetic Code

Our bodies are complex systems designed by God for health and longevity. But the chemicals and toxins found in processed foods are causing irreparable damage to our DNA.

- Bisphenol-A (BPA), used in food packaging, has been linked to mutations and alterations in the DNA structure.

- Acrylamide, a chemical formed when foods are cooked at high temperatures (like frying), has been shown to cause cancer in animal studies.
- Artificial sweeteners, such as aspartame, interfere with the body's natural metabolic processes, altering the expression of genes involved in appetite regulation and fat storage.

This genetic manipulation compromises the body's natural ability to heal, regenerate, and thrive.

10.3 The Gut-Brain Connection: A Toxic Relationship

The gut microbiome, the trillions of bacteria, fungi, and viruses in our digestive system, plays a crucial role in our overall health. However, the shift from whole foods to processed foods has disrupted this delicate balance. Processed foods, especially those high in sugar and fat, promote the growth of harmful bacteria, leading to:

- Leaky gut (intestinal permeability)
- Chronic inflammation
- Dysregulated hormones

This disruption also affects the brain. Over 90% of serotonin, the "feel-good" neurotransmitter, is produced in the gut. A damaged microbiome leads to:

- Anxiety
- Depression
- Mood swings

- Brain fog

This gut-brain connection reveals how what we eat impacts our emotional and cognitive health, which then affects our behaviour and worldview.

10.4 The Cancer Link: Processed Foods as Carcinogens

Processed foods, laden with artificial ingredients, preservatives, and trans fats, are directly linked to an increased risk of cancer. Some of the most concerning ingredients include:

- Nitrates and nitrites: Used to preserve processed meats like bacon, sausage, and hot dogs, these chemicals form carcinogenic compounds in the body.
- Caramel colouring: Found in sodas and packaged snacks, has been shown to cause lung cancer in animal studies.
- Artificial sweeteners: Studies have indicated that aspartame and saccharin may increase the risk of bladder cancer.

The more processed the food, the greater the risk of cell mutation, tumour growth, and organ damage.

10.5 Infertility and Hormonal Disruption: The Silent Epidemic

Many processed foods contain endocrine-disrupting chemicals, which interfere with the body's hormone systems.

These chemicals, such as phthalates and BPA, are found in the packaging and ingredients of processed foods. The effects on fertility are startling:

- Infertility rates are rising globally, especially in women who consume diets high in processed foods.
- Male sperm counts have been declining, partially due to exposure to chemicals that mimic oestrogen, disrupting the natural hormonal balance.

Processed foods short-circuit the body's reproductive system, leading to delayed pregnancies, complications, and even genetic mutations passed down to future generations.

10.6 Mental Health: The Hidden Cost of Junk Food

Processed foods are wreaking havoc not only on our bodies but on our minds. The ingredients in processed food have been linked to an increase in mental health disorders, including:

- Anxiety
- Depression
- Attention deficit disorders
- Memory loss

This occurs through the disruption of neurotransmitter production and the destruction of the blood-brain barrier, which is responsible for protecting the brain from harmful substances. The toxic combination of sugar, artificial additives, and unhealthy fats shuts down the body's natural defences, resulting in cognitive dysfunction and emotional instability.

10.7 Spiritual Numbness: Dulling Our Sensitivity to God

There is an often-overlooked aspect to the consumption of processed foods: spiritual numbness. Our physical state affects our spiritual sensitivity. *"Do you not know that your bodies are temples of the Holy Spirit, who is in you, whom you have received from God?"* — 1 Corinthians 6:19 NIV. Processed foods desensitise the body and mind to the Holy Spirit's promptings. Overeating sugar or consuming chemical-laden foods can dull:

- Our discernment
- Our convictions
- Our zeal for God's Word

Just as the body is an instrument for worship, it becomes a stumbling block when compromised by harmful substances. The more we feed our flesh, the less we hunger for the things of the Spirit.

10.8 A Call to Health: Reclaiming the Eden Blueprint

The evidence is clear. Processed foods are not simply a matter of taste or convenience; they are a silent epidemic that is destroying our bodies, minds, and spirits. But there is hope. We must return to the Eden Blueprint, where food is treated with reverence, care, and purpose. Choosing whole foods, growing our own produce, and rejecting toxic ingredients are practical steps that can restore our bodies to health. *"I am the bread of life. Whoever comes to me will never go hungry, and whoever believes in me will never be thirsty."* — John 6:35 NIV. God offers us life through His creation, not death through the processed imitation of man.

Final Reflection: What's on Your Plate?

In the next chapter, we will look at practical steps to reclaim our health, reverse the damage of processed foods, and restore our connection with God's divine plan for our bodies. The journey back to health begins with the simple question: What's on your plate?

Chapter 11

Rebuilding Health from the Ground Up
Practical Steps for Restoration

The destruction of health caused by processed foods is not a fate we must accept. Though the food industry has waged war on our bodies, minds, and spirits, we still have the power to reclaim our health and restore our lives to the way God intended. In this chapter, we'll explore practical steps to rebuild our physical, mental, and spiritual health by returning to God's design for food and holistic well-being. By embracing whole, nourishing foods and adopting a lifestyle rooted in biblical principles, we can reverse the damage caused by processed foods and restore our relationship with our Creator.

11.1 Returning to Eden: The Original Blueprint for Health

In the Garden of Eden, God's plan for human nourishment was clear: whole, natural foods that promote health and vitality. There were no additives, no preservatives, no genetically modified crops, just the pure, life-giving produce of creation. *"Then God said, 'I give you every seed-bearing plant on the face*

of the whole earth and every tree that has fruit with seed in it.
They will be yours for food." — Genesis 1:29 NIV. God's design
for our nourishment is simple but profound. It is built on the
principle of wholeness, where food serves as both sustenance
and medicine. When we eat what God intended, whole,
unprocessed, life-giving foods, we align our bodies with His
design and honour Him with our physical health.

11.2 The Power of Whole Foods: Reclaiming Our Health

To restore our health, we must focus on the foods God created
for us. Whole foods are not only more nutritious; they also
help the body detoxify, heal, and regenerate.

1. **Fruits and Vegetables:** The cornerstone of any healing
   diet. These nutrient-dense foods provide essential
   vitamins, minerals, and antioxidants that support the
   body's detoxification processes and repair mechanisms.
   o Leafy greens like spinach, kale, and chard provide
     high amounts of magnesium, a mineral that supports
     nerve function and relaxation.
   o Berries are rich in antioxidants, particularly
     flavonoids, which help to reduce inflammation and
     fight oxidative stress.
2. **Whole Grains:** Unlike refined grains, whole grains like
   quinoa, brown rice, and oats are rich in fibre, which
   supports gut health and stabilises blood sugar levels.
3. **Nuts and Seeds:** Packed with healthy fats, these foods
   support brain function, hormone balance, and
   cardiovascular health. Focus on almonds, walnuts, chia
   seeds, and flaxseeds.

4. **Lean Protein:** Animal protein from grass-fed meats, wild-caught fish, and organic eggs is rich in essential amino acids necessary for tissue repair, muscle growth, and overall vitality.

5. **Healthy Fats:** Incorporating natural fats such as avocados, olive oil, and coconut oil can improve brain health, reduce inflammation, and support hormone balance.

6. **Herbs and Spices:** Turmeric, ginger, garlic, and cinnamon are powerful tools in fighting inflammation, boosting immunity, and promoting digestion.

By focusing on these foods, we nourish our bodies in a way that processed foods simply cannot. These foods strengthen the immune system, regulate metabolism, and help to repair the damage caused by years of poor eating habits.

11.3 Detoxifying Your Body: Cleansing and Healing

To truly reclaim health, we must not only nourish our bodies but also detoxify and cleanse the toxins that have accumulated over time due to a diet of processed foods.

1. **Drink Water:** Staying hydrated is essential for flushing toxins from the body. Aim for at least 8 glasses of water per day, and consider adding lemon or apple cider vinegar to help alkalise the body.

2. **Intermittent Fasting:** Fasting gives the digestive system a break, allowing the body to focus on repair and regeneration. Start with a 12-hour fast (for example,

eating from 7 a.m. to 7 p.m.) and gradually increase the fasting window as your body becomes accustomed.

3. **Eat Detoxifying Foods:** In addition to whole foods, certain foods support the body's detoxification processes:
   o Cilantro helps to eliminate heavy metals.
   o Beets stimulate liver detoxification and improve digestion.
   o Green tea is rich in antioxidants that support the liver's natural detox process.

4. **Exercise:** Physical movement promotes lymphatic drainage and enhances detoxification. Aim for at least 30 minutes of moderate exercise a day, whether through walking, swimming, or yoga.

5. **Sleep:** Sleep is one of the most vital ways the body heals. Aim for 7-9 hours of quality sleep each night to allow the body to repair itself and flush toxins during the night.

11.4 Emotional and Mental Restoration: Feeding the Mind

What we eat affects our mental state, and restoring our physical health goes hand in hand with restoring our mental well-being.

1. **The Power of Prayer:** Every restoration begins in the spirit. Use prayer to commit your health journey to God, asking Him to guide your steps and strengthen your willpower.

2. **Meditation and Mindfulness:** Just as we need to nourish our bodies, we must also take time to nourish our minds. Spending time in silent reflection, meditation on

Scripture, or mindfulness can reduce stress, improve focus, and restore emotional balance.

3. **Gratitude:** Cultivating a grateful heart for the food we eat and the body we've been given enhances our overall well-being. Practice gratitude for the simple, healthy meals you prepare.

4. **Limit Toxic Inputs:** Just as we must be mindful of what we put in our bodies, we must be discerning about what we put into our minds. Limit exposure to negative news, toxic media, and environments that hinder your mental peace.

11.5 Spiritual Healing: Returning to God's Purpose for Our Bodies

Our health is not just a physical matter; it is a spiritual act of stewardship. Caring for our bodies is an expression of our devotion to God.

1. **Honor God with Your Body:** As Christians, we are called to treat our bodies as temples of the Holy Spirit. Eating nourishing foods, exercising, and resting are all ways we can honour God with our physical being. *"Therefore, whether you eat or drink, or whatever you do, do all to the glory of God."* — 1 Corinthians 10:31 NIV.

2. **Reject the Lies of the Enemy:** The enemy seeks to steal, kill, and destroy, which includes our physical, mental, and spiritual health. Reject the lies that processed foods and unhealthy habits are normal or acceptable. Choose life!

3. **Cultivate Community:** Join a group of like-minded believers who support your health journey. Whether it's a

local church group, a Bible study, or a health-focused community, accountability and encouragement are vital for long-term success.

11.6 Practical Steps to Get Started

1. **Start Small:** Begin by eliminating the most toxic foods in your diet (e.g., soda, packaged snacks, fast food) and replace them with whole food options.
2. **Meal Planning:** Plan your meals ahead of time to avoid the temptation of reaching for processed food when you're hungry.
3. **Cooking from Scratch:** Start cooking meals from fresh, whole ingredients. Begin with simple recipes that require minimal ingredients and progress from there.
4. **Shop Smart:** Focus on buying fresh produce, grass-fed meats, and whole grains. Avoid the centre aisles of the grocery store, where processed foods are typically located.
5. **Pray Over Your Food:** Every meal is an opportunity to honour God. Pray for the food, for health, and for gratitude.

Final Reflection: Restoring the Body, Mind, and Spirit

Health is more than just a physical state; it's a holistic pursuit that involves the body, mind, and spirit. By returning to God's original plan for nourishment, we can reverse the damage caused by processed foods and restore our health in every area of life. It's time to reclaim the Eden blueprint for living and reject the lie of convenience over health. With every step we take towards health, we move closer to the life that God intended for us, a life of vitality, peace, and purpose.

Chapter 12

The Global Food Crisis
From Eden to Global Dependency

The world is facing an unprecedented crisis: food insecurity and the globalisation of unhealthy eating patterns. The very systems that were meant to sustain us are now contributing to the destruction of our health, the ravaging of our planet, and the enslaving of nations to a toxic cycle of dependency. As the industrialisation of agriculture and the dominance of processed foods grow, we are witnessing a global shift away from Eden's perfect design to a broken and unsustainable food system. In this chapter, we will explore the origins of the worldwide food crisis, the consequences of our current agricultural and food systems, and how this crisis can be traced back to the loss of God's original blueprint for nourishment. Through this exploration, we will gain a deeper understanding of why the modern food system is harming us and the world, and how we can turn the tide by returning to Eden's model.

12.1 The Industrialisation of Food: A Shift from Life to Death

The global food system has undergone a radical transformation in the past century. Once, farming was a practice that connected people with the earth and with the Creator. However, the rise of industrial farming has separated humans from nature, turning food into a commodity rather than a gift.

1. **Monoculture and GMOs:** Industrial farming practices emphasise monoculture, the cultivation of a single crop over large swaths of land. This has led to the widespread use of genetically modified organisms (GMOs) and chemical fertilisers to increase crop yields, often at the expense of soil health. The practice of monoculture reduces biodiversity, makes crops more susceptible to pests, and requires heavy use of chemical pesticides and herbicides, which in turn poison the environment and those who consume the crops.

2. **The Mechanisation of Food Production:** The shift from traditional farming methods to mechanised food production has led to a decline in the quality of food. Massive factory farms prioritise efficiency and profitability over the well-being of animals, workers, and consumers. The conditions in these factory farms often lead to the spread of diseases like E. coli and Salmonella, which are then transmitted to consumers through the consumption of contaminated meat.

3. **The Rise of Processed Foods:** The most insidious aspect of the global food crisis is the prevalence of processed foods. Highly refined and chemically altered, these foods are designed to be cheap, convenient, and shelf-stable, but they often lack the nutritional value and vitality of whole,

natural foods. Additives, preservatives, and artificial sweeteners have replaced the wholesome ingredients of God's design, leading to a population plagued with obesity, diabetes, heart disease, and cancer.

4. **The Globalisation of Junk Food:** What began as a problem in developed nations has now spread worldwide. The globalisation of fast-food chains and the proliferation of ultra-processed, junk food products have created a worldwide epidemic of poor nutrition. As countries around the globe adopt Western eating habits, they are facing the same health challenges that plague the developed world: increased rates of chronic disease, economic instability, and food dependency.

12.2 The Environmental Cost: The Destruction of God's Creation

The effects of industrial agriculture are not just felt in the health of individuals; they also have devastating consequences for the environment. The very land that was created to provide for humanity has been exploited and degraded in the pursuit of profit.

1. **Soil Degradation:** The overuse of chemical fertilisers and the practice of monoculture have led to widespread soil depletion. Healthy soil is the foundation of sustainable farming, but industrial farming practices are stripping the land of its nutrients, leading to lower crop yields and environmental pollution.

2. **Deforestation:** As demand for crops like soy and palm oil increases, forests are being cleared at alarming rates to

make way for industrial agriculture. This destruction of forests contributes to biodiversity loss, climate change, and the displacement of indigenous populations.

3. **Water Pollution and Scarcity:** The use of chemical fertilisers and pesticides contaminates water supplies, polluting rivers and lakes and harming aquatic life. Meanwhile, industrial farming practices are often water-intensive, contributing to the overuse of freshwater resources, further exacerbating the global water crisis.

4. **Greenhouse Gas Emissions:** The industrial food system is a significant contributor to climate change, responsible for a large portion of global greenhouse gas emissions. From the transportation of food products across the globe to the methane emissions from factory farming, the modern food system is a major driver of global warming.

12.3 The Moral and Ethical Crisis: The Exploitation of Humanity

The global food crisis is not only an environmental issue but also a moral and ethical issue. The industrial food system has created a world where the rich get richer while the poor are left to suffer.

1. **Exploitation of Workers:** The labour force behind the industrial food system often works under inhumane conditions. Migrant workers on factory farms and in meatpacking plants are often subjected to long hours, low wages, and dangerous working environments. They are treated as mere cogs in a machine, rather than valued human beings.

2. **Food Insecurity:** Ironically, even though the world produces more food than ever before, billions of people still suffer from hunger and food insecurity. This is largely due to the inequitable distribution of food, where wealthier nations consume a disproportionate share of the world's resources, leaving the poorest to fend for themselves with limited access to nutritious, life-sustaining food.

3. **The Power of Big Agriculture:** A handful of multinational corporations dominate the global food industry, wielding immense power over the food supply. These companies prioritise profits over people, and their control over the food chain leads to monopolies, price manipulation, and the disempowerment of local farmers. This has resulted in the near destruction of small-scale agriculture, which has historically been a vital part of global food security.

12.4 The Return to Eden: A Call to Action

The global food crisis reflects our departure from God's original plan for food. However, there is hope. By returning to the Eden model, a model of holistic, sustainable agriculture rooted in natural, unprocessed foods, we can begin to heal both our bodies and the world.

1. **Support Sustainable Farming:** Choose to support local, sustainable farmers who use natural methods of farming and prioritise the health of the soil, animals, and people. This will help promote a food system that honours God's

creation and reduces the environmental impact of industrial agriculture.

2. **Embrace Whole, Unprocessed Foods:** Reject the modern food system's emphasis on processed foods and return to whole, natural foods. Shop at farmers' markets, grow your own food if possible, and educate others on the importance of eating God's natural provisions.

3. **Advocate for Fair Food Systems:** We must work together to create a food system that is just and equitable, one where everyone has access to nutritious, life-giving food. Support policies that encourage local food production, fair trade, and ethical farming practices.

4. **Pray for Global Healing:** The global food crisis is a spiritual issue, and we must pray for God to heal the land, restore food systems, and bring His provision to all nations. Ask God to guide you in making choices that honour Him with your food choices.

Final Reflection: Reclaiming the Table

The modern food system has led humanity down a dangerous path. But as believers, we know that God is in the business of restoration. By returning to His original blueprint for food, we can begin to rebuild a healthy, sustainable world, a world where we honour God with our bodies, our resources, and our relationships with others. The road to healing is not easy, but it begins with a simple choice: to embrace Eden's model of food, reject the forces of industrialisation, and seek to honour God in every bite. It's time for us to take responsibility for our health, our environment, and our fellow man, and to work together to heal the brokenness of our food systems.

Chapter 13

Building Sustainable Food Communities
A Biblical Approach to Local Food Security

In the previous chapter, we discussed the global food crisis and its devastating effects on health, the environment, and society. Now, we turn our attention to solutions. In this chapter, we will explore how we can build sustainable food communities that not only support the health of individuals and families but also contribute to the restoration of God's creation. By looking at local food security through a biblical lens, we will see that God's design for food is rooted in community, stewardship, and justice.

13.1 The Biblical Mandate for Community and Stewardship

From the beginning of creation, God's intention was for humanity to live in relationship with Him and with one another. In Eden, food was abundant, healthy, and accessible to all. It was a divine provision designed to sustain life, but it was also part of a larger picture of community and stewardship.

1. **God's Provision for All:** In Genesis 1:29, God said, *"Behold, I have given you every herb bearing seed, which is upon the face of all the earth, and every tree, in which is the fruit of a tree yielding seed; to you it shall be for meat."* This command was not just about nourishment—it was about God's generosity and His desire for all of humanity to have access to good, healthy food. Food was to be a gift, meant to be shared and enjoyed in community.

2. **Stewardship of the Earth:** In Genesis 2:15, God placed Adam in the Garden of Eden to tend and keep it. This speaks to humanity's role as stewards of the earth. The earth was entrusted to Adam to care for, cultivate, and protect. This principle of stewardship extends to how we interact with the land, how we manage natural resources, and how we care for the creatures that inhabit it.

3. **The Concept of Jubilee:** In the Old Testament, the Year of Jubilee (Leviticus 25) was a time when land was returned to its original owners, debts were forgiven, and all people had access to the resources they needed. This was a way of ensuring that no one would be left without. It was a biblical model of food justice, one that ensured the land and its produce were shared by all, not hoarded by the wealthy or powerful.

13.2 Building Local Food Systems — A Return to Community-Based Agriculture

As we face the global food crisis, one of the most effective solutions is to focus on local food systems. These systems prioritise small-scale, sustainable farming that feeds local communities and supports the economy while honouring God's creation.

1. **Community-Supported Agriculture (CSA):** One way to build local food security is through community-supported agriculture (CSA), where individuals or families purchase shares in a farm's seasonal produce. This model ensures that farmers have a steady income, and consumers receive fresh, local produce. It also encourages community involvement in food production and helps create stronger connections between the people who grow food and the people who consume it.

2. **Urban Farming and Permaculture:** Cities around the world are discovering the benefits of urban farming, growing food within city limits on rooftops, vacant lots, and even in backyards. Permaculture practices, which emphasise designing sustainable and self-sufficient agricultural systems, can be implemented in urban areas to create resilient local food systems. These practices also encourage the use of companion planting, organic farming, and the restoration of soil health.

3. **Cooperative Farming Models:** Another approach to local food security is the development of food cooperatives, businesses owned and operated by the community. These cooperatives can be involved in growing, distributing, and selling local produce. By working together, individuals can reduce the cost of food, support local farmers, and ensure the availability of fresh, healthy food in their communities.

4. **Food Sovereignty:** A key concept in building sustainable food communities is food sovereignty, which emphasises

the right of communities to control their own food systems. It's about democratising food production and ensuring that local populations have access to the resources, knowledge, and land needed to feed themselves. This means reducing dependency on multinational corporations and large-scale industrial farming and instead focusing on community-based solutions.

13.3 Biblical Principles for Local Food Security

The Bible offers practical wisdom for building food security at the local level. By looking at the principles in Scripture, we can find inspiration for cultivating a food system that honours both God and people.

1. **Sharing and Generosity:** In Acts 2:44-45 NIV, we see the early Church exemplifying the practice of sharing: *"All the believers were together and had everything in common. They sold property and possessions to give to anyone who had need."* This is the biblical model of generosity, a model where food, resources, and wealth are shared within the community. Building local food systems based on this principle of sharing ensures that everyone's needs are met and that no one is left hungry.

2. **Sabbath Rest for the Land:** God instructed His people to allow the land to rest every seventh year (Leviticus 25:4 NIV). This command was not just about spiritual rest but also about renewing the land. This principle is relevant today as we look to practices like crop rotation and cover cropping, which allow the soil to regenerate and maintain

its fertility. In sustainable food systems, the land must be allowed to rest to avoid depletion and preserve its long-term productivity.

3. **Work and Labour:** In Genesis 2:15 NIV, God gives Adam the task of tending and keeping the garden; this is a call to work in partnership with God to care for His creation. In local food systems, the value of hard work and honouring the land is key. It requires sacrifice, dedication, and labour, but also brings satisfaction, sustenance, and community well-being.

4. **Justice and Fairness:** God is a God of justice, and throughout Scripture, we see His concern for the marginalised and poor (Proverbs 31:8-9 NIV). A sustainable food system must promote justice for all people, particularly for small-scale farmers, local communities, and those living in food deserts. Fair wages, equitable access to resources, and responsible trade practices are central to building a food system that honours the biblical principles of justice.

13.4 Practical Steps for Building Food Security in Your Community

Building a sustainable, food-secure community begins with individuals taking practical steps toward creating change. Here are several ways you can start:

1. **Start a Garden:** Whether you have a small backyard or an apartment balcony, growing your own food is one of the most impactful ways to reclaim your food security. Start with simple vegetables, herbs, and fruits. Not only does it

reduce dependence on commercial food systems, but it also brings a sense of fulfilment and connection with God's creation.

2. **Support Local Farmers and Markets:** Purchase food from local farmers' markets, food cooperatives, or community-supported agriculture programs. By supporting these local food sources, you are encouraging sustainability and ensuring that your money goes directly to small-scale producers rather than corporate food giants.

3. **Educate Your Community:** Share knowledge about the importance of sustainable food practices with your community. Hold workshops on gardening, healthy eating, and food preservation. By educating others, you can help create a culture of food security that encourages healthier choices and more sustainable practices.

4. **Advocate for Policy Change:** Get involved in advocating for policies that support local food systems and food sovereignty. This might include supporting small farmers, reducing government subsidies for industrial agriculture, or pushing for better food distribution networks in underserved areas.

Final Reflection: Embracing the Fullness of God's Provision

The world is facing a food crisis, but the solution lies in returning to God's design for food, a design that celebrates community, stewardship, and justice. By building local food systems that honour these biblical principles, we can create a sustainable future where all people have access to nourishing, life-giving food. It is time for us to take responsibility for our food systems, to embrace God's call to stewardship, and to work together to restore the brokenness of the global food crisis.

Chapter 14

Creating a Movement of Change
Empowering Communities for Global Food Restoration

As we have explored in previous chapters, the global food crisis is a result of centuries of industrialisation, exploitation, and neglect of God's original design for food and the earth. But within this crisis lies an opportunity, a chance for restoration. The question is, how can we, as individuals, communities, and nations, create a movement of change that addresses the root causes of the global food disaster and returns us to the principles laid out by God for the flourishing of humanity? In this chapter, we will explore how to empower communities to act and restore their food systems, focusing on biblical principles that can guide us in creating sustainable, just, and equitable food systems. This chapter will show that the movement for change is not only possible but essential if we are to fulfil God's call to care for the earth and ensure that future generations can live with access to healthy, nutritious food.

14.1 The Power of Community Action

Throughout history, great movements of change have started with small, local communities that came together to take action on issues they were passionate about. This has never been truer than in the fight for global food restoration. While governments and corporations may play significant roles, the most profound and lasting change begins in our local communities.

1. **Local Movements Leading to Global Change:** In the face of global challenges, local movements have shown incredible power to impact broader systemic change. From the slow food movement to urban gardening projects, individuals and communities around the world are choosing to take control of their food sources and work toward sustainable practices. These small-scale efforts often ripple outwards, inspiring neighbouring communities and eventually catching the attention of policymakers.

2. **Unity in Purpose:** The key to this local movement is the unity of purpose, when communities come together with a shared vision, there is a collective power that can lead to transformation. By uniting around a shared goal, such as restoring sustainable farming practices or advocating for local food security, communities can mobilise resources, engage decision-makers, and encourage others to join the cause.

3. **Collaboration and Partnership:** Empowering communities for food restoration is not about isolated efforts. It is about building collaborations between farmers, consumers, faith communities, local governments, and businesses. Partnerships that bring

different perspectives and expertise to the table will be key in building sustainable local food systems.

14.2 Biblical Vision for Empowering Communities

As we turn to the Bible, we see that God has always intended for His people to work together in community to care for the earth and one another. Here are some key biblical principles that can guide us in empowering communities for global food restoration:

1. **The Power of One — The Parable of the Mustard Seed:** Jesus teaches us in Matthew 13:31-32 that the kingdom of God is like a mustard seed, small yet capable of growing into something great. In the same way, the smallest act of faith, no matter how insignificant it may seem, can grow into a powerful force for change. The movement for food restoration may start with one person or a small group of people, but with God's blessing, it can expand and impact the entire world.

2. **Caring for the Least of These:** In Matthew 25:40, Jesus says, *"Whatever you did for one of the least of these brothers and sisters of mine, you did for me."* Food justice is a matter of caring for the marginalised, the poor, and the hungry. Empowering communities to restore their food systems is not just about improving the health of individuals; it is about ensuring that all people, especially the vulnerable, have access to the resources they need to thrive. This is a biblical call to justice that requires us to look beyond our own needs and focus on those who are most affected by the food crisis.

3. **The Year of Jubilee — A Vision for Restoration:** As we discussed in Chapter 13, the Year of Jubilee (Leviticus 25) is a time when land is restored, debts are forgiven, and justice is pursued. This biblical principle of restoration is relevant today as we look at how we can restore broken food systems. It is a vision of renewal, of returning to a state of balance and equity. Empowering communities for global food restoration means giving them the tools and the vision for justice and restoration in their local contexts.

4. **Multiplying Resources:** In Matthew 14:13-21, Jesus fed the 5,000 with five loaves and two fish. The miracle is not just in the multiplication of the food, it is in the faith that God can take what we have, no matter how small, and multiply it for the good of others. In the same way, empowering communities to restore local food security requires faith. Faith that God will use the resources at our disposal, even if they seem small, to meet the needs of all.

14.3 Practical Steps for Building a Movement of Change

Creating a global movement of food restoration requires action. It is not enough to simply talk about the problems we face; we must act. Here are practical steps that individuals and communities can take to build a movement of change for global food restoration:

1. **Raise Awareness:** The first step in creating a movement of change is to raise awareness. Inform your community about the issues facing the global food system, such as the dangers of processed food, the impact of industrial

agriculture, and the need for food justice. Share resources, host discussions, and engage people in understanding the importance of food security.

2. **Get Involved in Local Food Projects:** There are likely already efforts in your community aimed at improving food security. Get involved with community gardens, farmers' markets, and sustainable food initiatives. If these efforts don't exist, consider starting one! Encourage others to join you in developing local food systems that emphasise sustainability and justice.

3. **Advocate for Change:** Start advocating for policies that support local food systems and food sovereignty. Write letters to local government officials, attend meetings, and use your voice to push for just food policies. Encourage others in your community to do the same.

4. **Form Partnerships and Coalitions:** Building a movement requires collaboration. Seek out like-minded individuals and organisations to join forces in working toward common goals. By working together, we can amplify our impact and create a more powerful movement for global food restoration.

5. **Educate and Equip the Next Generation:** Empower the next generation by teaching them about sustainable farming practices, food justice, and the biblical principles of stewardship. By equipping young people with the knowledge and tools to lead, we can ensure that this movement will continue long into the future.

14.4 Conclusion: A Vision for Global Restoration

The global food crisis is a challenge, but it is also an opportunity to return to God's design for food and creation.

By empowering communities to take action, we can restore what has been broken and transform the global food system. This movement is not just about better farming practices or healthier food choices; it is about creating a world where all people can experience the abundant life that God intended for us. It is about community, stewardship, and justice. And it is about working together, as individuals and communities, to build a food system that reflects God's goodness and care for all creation. As we conclude this book, I encourage you to join the movement. Whether through small, local actions or large-scale advocacy, you have the power to make a difference. The restoration of the global food system begins with you.

Chapter 15

Overcoming Resistance
Addressing the Challenges to Food Restoration

As we have discussed throughout this book, the global food crisis is a complex and deeply ingrained issue, and the road to food restoration is not without its obstacles. Despite the clear need for change and the biblical mandate to care for creation, there are powerful forces that resist efforts to restore the food system to a more sustainable and equitable state. In this chapter, we will explore the challenges and resistance that arise when advocating for food restoration and how we can address them. From the influence of big agriculture and processed food industries to the political and economic forces at play, there are many obstacles standing in the way of true food restoration. But these challenges are not insurmountable. By understanding the forces at work and staying true to our biblical values, we can overcome resistance and continue to push forward in the fight for a healthier, more sustainable food system.

15.1 The Power of Big Agriculture and Processed Food Industries

One of the most significant sources of resistance to food restoration is the power and influence of large agricultural corporations and the processed food industry. These industries have long controlled the global food system, shaping production practices, marketing strategies, and even government policies to suit their interests.

1. **The Economic Interests of Big Agriculture:** Industrial agriculture, dominated by a few multinational corporations, has long prioritised profit over the well-being of the environment and human health. These corporations use their economic power to influence policy, control food production, and monopolise the market. They often lobby governments to subsidise harmful farming practices that promote monoculture, chemical use, and environmental degradation.

2. **The Processed Food Industry:** The rise of processed foods, particularly ultra-processed and junk foods, has been a key driver of the global health crisis. These foods are often cheap to produce and highly profitable, but they are also nutritionally poor and contribute to a variety of chronic diseases. The processed food industry spends billions of dollars annually on marketing and advertising, creating a culture that encourages unhealthy eating and undermines efforts to promote healthy, natural foods.

3. **The Global Reach of These Industries:** The scale of these industries is global, with a massive influence on both developed and developing countries. In many parts of the world, the dominance of processed food and industrial agriculture has led to the destruction of local food systems, the depletion of soil, and the erosion of

traditional farming practices. As a result, these industries create significant resistance to efforts aimed at restoring sustainable and healthy food practices.

15.2 Political and Economic Challenges

In addition to the influence of powerful industries, there are also significant political and economic challenges that hinder the progress of food restoration.

1. **Government Subsidies and Policies:** Governments around the world often subsidise the industrial agriculture system, making it financially advantageous for large corporations to continue with unsustainable practices. These subsidies create an economic environment in which small, local farmers struggle to compete, and the push for food restoration is met with resistance from policymakers who are invested in the status quo.

2. **Global Trade Agreements and the Free Market:** Global trade agreements and the promotion of free-market policies often prioritise economic growth over environmental and health concerns. These policies frequently make it difficult for countries to regulate or ban harmful food practices, as trade deals often impose legal barriers that prevent governments from taking strong action to protect their citizens' health.

3. **The Economic Costs of Change:** Restoring a sustainable food system requires investment in new farming practices, community-based food systems, and education. However, the shift away from industrialised food systems

can appear costly, especially in the short term. For many communities, particularly those in developing countries, the transition to sustainable agriculture may seem like an economic burden that they cannot afford. Overcoming this challenge requires financial support, government incentives, and market incentives that make it easier for communities to invest in sustainable food systems.

4. **The Influence of the Media:** The media plays a critical role in shaping public opinion. However, the food industry has vast resources to influence the media, often promoting misinformation about the benefits of processed foods or minimising the harm caused by industrial agriculture. This media manipulation can create confusion among the public and hinder efforts to advocate for food restoration.

15.3 Cultural and Behavioural Resistance

While political and economic challenges are significant, there are also cultural and behavioural factors that contribute to resistance. Changing people's eating habits and mindsets is no small feat, especially when they have been conditioned over decades to consume processed foods.

1. **Convenience and Accessibility:** Processed foods are often marketed as convenient and affordable. In a fast-paced world, people are drawn to foods that require little preparation and are easy to access. This preference for convenience makes it difficult to encourage people to adopt healthier, more sustainable eating habits.

2. **Cultural Norms and Habits:** Food is deeply ingrained in culture, tradition, and daily routines. People are often resistant to change when it comes to their food choices because they are tied to emotions, memories, and identity. Breaking these cultural ties to processed foods can be a major obstacle in efforts to restore food systems.

3. **Lack of Education:** Many people are not aware of the long-term health consequences of eating processed foods or the environmental damage caused by industrial agriculture. Without education about the benefits of sustainable and healthy food choices, people may resist changing their eating habits, even if they are motivated to do so.

15.4 Overcoming Resistance: Strategies for Change

While the challenges outlined above are substantial, they are not insurmountable. Here are some strategies that can help overcome resistance and push the movement for food restoration forward:

1. **Education and Advocacy:** Educating the public about the dangers of processed foods and the benefits of a sustainable food system is crucial. Utilise platforms such as social media, community events, and local schools to raise awareness about food justice, healthy eating, and the importance of restoring God's design for food.

2. **Support for Local Farmers and Producers:** Advocate for policies that support local food systems and provide financial support to small-scale farmers who use sustainable farming practices. Promote farmers' markets,

community-supported agriculture (CSA), and local food initiatives that provide alternatives to industrialised food systems.

3. **Policy Reform:** Work toward changing government policies that support industrial agriculture and processed foods. Advocate for stronger regulations on food labelling, restrictions on unhealthy food marketing, and subsidies for sustainable farming.

4. **Building Community Movements:** Start or join local food initiatives that encourage community-based food systems, such as urban farming, food cooperatives, and community gardens. Empower people to take control of their own food production and build networks of support.

5. **Faith-Based Advocacy:** Leverage the power of faith communities to advocate for food justice. Faith leaders can help spread the message of stewardship, sustainability, and justice, and encourage congregations to make food choices that reflect biblical values.

15.5 Conclusion: Persevering in the Face of Resistance

The road to food restoration will undoubtedly be met with resistance from many sources, corporations, governments, cultural norms, and economic systems. But with faith, determination, and collaboration, we can overcome these challenges and create a food system that aligns with God's original design for creation. The key is to stay the course and remain committed to the principles of justice, sustainability, and community. In the face of resistance, we must remember the words of the Apostle Paul: *"Let us not become weary in doing good, for at the proper time we will reap a harvest if we do not give up"* (Galatians 6:9). The movement for food restoration may be challenging, but with perseverance and faith, we can overcome resistance and build a better, healthier future for all of creation.

Chapter 16

A Call to Action
Restoring the Land and Our Lives

As we have explored throughout this book, the modern food system is broken, and its consequences are dire. Processed foods are contributing to a global health crisis, and the industrial agriculture that supports them is degrading the very soil that sustains life. But we do not have to accept this reality. We are called to action, to restore the land, to care for creation, and to return to God's original design for food and health. This chapter will explore practical steps for food restoration, both at the individual level and in the broader context of society. We will also discuss the spiritual foundation for this movement, drawing on biblical principles that call us to stewardship and community.

16.1 A Biblical Foundation for Food Restoration

The restoration of food systems is not just a matter of environmentalism or health; it is deeply spiritual. The Bible speaks clearly about our responsibility as stewards of the earth, entrusted by God to care for His creation. Our relationship with food is an extension of our relationship with God, and how we treat the land and our bodies reflects our reverence for His design.

1. **The Call to Stewardship:** From the very beginning, God gave humanity the responsibility to care for the earth. In Genesis 1:28, He commanded Adam and Eve to "fill the earth and subdue it," and in Genesis 2:15, He placed Adam in the Garden of Eden to work it and take care of it. This command to tend and cultivate the land was not just about survival but about maintaining the harmony between humanity and creation.

2. **The Sabbath Rest for the Land:** God also established the concept of the Sabbath not only for people but for the land. Leviticus 25:4 reveals that every seventh year, the land was to have a Sabbath rest. This law demonstrates the importance of renewing and resting the soil, a practice that is now largely neglected in modern agriculture, where constant use and depletion of the earth's resources are the norm.

3. **God's Provision in the Garden:** The Garden of Eden was abundant and diverse, full of trees bearing fruit and plants for food (Genesis 2:9). God's original plan was for humanity to live in harmony with creation, eating the natural foods He provided. The simplicity and wholesomeness of the Garden's produce were meant to nourish both the body and the soul.

4. **Jesus and the Kingdom of God:** In the teachings of Jesus, there are numerous references to the Kingdom of God being like a seed or a vineyard (Matthew 13:31-33). These metaphors emphasise the idea of growth, cultivation, and

the need for careful tending of the earth. Jesus also taught about the importance of health and wholeness, both spiritually and physically. He healed the sick, fed the hungry, and showed that God's Kingdom is a place of abundance, peace, and restoration.

16.2 Practical Steps for Food Restoration

Food restoration is a comprehensive effort that involves many facets, from changing what we eat to altering how food is produced. The steps below outline practical ways we can participate in this movement and begin restoring our food systems.

1. **Eating Whole, Unprocessed Foods:** The most immediate action individuals can take is to shift toward a whole foods diet. This means eating fruits, vegetables, whole grains, legumes, and nutritious animal products that are minimally processed. By choosing whole foods, we support the restoration of local food systems and avoid the harmful effects of ultra-processed foods.

2. **Support Local Farmers and Sustainable Agriculture:** Instead of relying on industrial agriculture, seek out local farmers who use sustainable farming practices. Support community-based agriculture, farmers' markets, and community-supported agriculture (CSA) programs. These models promote soil health, biodiversity, and the well-being of both farmers and consumers.

3. **Grow Your Own Food:** Even if you don't have a large space, growing your own food is one of the most effective ways to restore the land and take control of your food

sources. Start with a small garden or even container gardening. By growing food at home, you engage in a process of connection with the land and a deeper understanding of where your food comes from.

4. **Compost and Recycle:** Reducing food waste and creating a closed-loop system in your own home can help restore the earth's fertility. Composting organic materials and using them to nourish your garden is a practical way to care for the land while reducing waste. Additionally, make efforts to reduce your overall consumption of packaged and processed foods.

5. **Advocate for Policy Change:** On a larger scale, support policies that promote sustainable agriculture, food sovereignty, and healthier food systems. Advocate for government subsidies for small-scale, sustainable farmers and push for stronger regulations on food labelling and marketing. Encourage your local government to create programs that support food justice and equity for all communities.

16.3 Restoring the Land and Our Lives: A Call to Action

The restoration of our food systems will not happen overnight, and it will not be easy. But with faith, determination, and action, we can make a significant difference. The biblical call to stewardship and care for the earth is more relevant today than ever before. As we work toward food restoration, we not only care for the land but also our health and well-being. This call to action is a holistic endeavour that involves every aspect of our lives. It's about more than just food; it's about restoring a way of life that aligns with God's original design for creation. It's about creating a world where we care for the earth, care for each other, and enjoy the abundance that God has provided in a way that reflects His love, justice, and peace. As we move forward, remember the words of the prophet Micah: *"He has shown you, O mortal, what is good. And what does the Lord require of you? To act justly and to love mercy and to walk humbly with your God"* (Micah 6:8 NIV). Acting justly, loving mercy, and walking humbly with God means caring for His creation and restoring the food systems that sustain life.

16.4 Conclusion: Moving Toward Restoration

The global genocide of the modern age, driven by the exploitation of food and agriculture systems, is a tragic reality. But there is hope. Through biblical principles, practical actions, and community-based efforts, we can begin the process of restoring both the land and our lives. It's time to return to the Edenic vision of a world where we live in harmony with creation and where our food nourishes us in body and soul. This is our call to action. Let us rise together and take the necessary steps to restore the land and our lives, for the future of our children and the generations to come.

Chapter 17

Reclaiming Our Health
The Battle Against Processed Foods

The modern world is witnessing an alarming rise in chronic diseases, conditions that were once rare but are now prevalent in nearly every nation. From heart disease and diabetes to cancer and obesity, these ailments have taken a devastating toll on human health. But the culprit behind this health crisis is not merely genetics or bad luck; it is the food we consume, particularly the proliferation of processed foods. Processed foods are defined as those that have been altered from their natural state through methods such as refining, preserving, artificial flavouring, and colouring. These foods often contain high levels of sugar, refined grains, trans fats, preservatives, and additives that contribute to a range of health problems. The convenience and affordability of these foods have made them a staple in the modern diet, but the hidden cost is far more than we realise. In this chapter, we will explore the relationship between processed foods and chronic diseases, examine how modern diets are eroding our health, and consider biblical principles that offer hope for healing and restoration.

17.1 The Rise of Processed Foods and the Decline of Health

Historically, human beings ate whole foods: fruits, vegetables, grains, and animal products that were as close to their natural state as possible. The agricultural revolution brought about changes in food production, but these changes were relatively slow and did not drastically alter the nutritional value of food. However, in the 20th century, food production underwent a seismic shift, and processed foods began to dominate the market. The advent of industrialised farming, mass production, and preservation techniques revolutionised the food industry, but at what cost? The excessive processing of food, which started with the advent of canning, pasteurisation, and artificial flavouring, has resulted in foods that are highly caloric yet nutritionally poor. Over time, these processed foods became more refined, leading to the creation of the ultra-processed foods that are common today. Ultra-processed foods are now the standard in many diets across the globe. These foods are cheap, convenient, and heavily marketed, making them highly accessible to people of all ages. Unfortunately, they are often addictive and offer little in the way of nutrition. The refined sugars, chemicals, and artificial additives in processed foods wreak havoc on our bodies.

The Connection Between Processed Foods and Chronic Diseases

Research shows a clear connection between processed foods and the rise of chronic diseases. Studies have demonstrated that diets rich in refined sugars, trans fats, and additives contribute to a wide range of health issues:

1. **Heart Disease:** The high levels of sodium, saturated fats, and trans fats found in processed foods are major contributors to the development of cardiovascular disease. These foods raise bad cholesterol levels and increase the risk of high blood pressure.
2. **Obesity:** The abundance of sugar and refined carbohydrates in processed foods leads to insulin resistance and weight gain. These foods are energy-dense but nutrient-poor, leading people to overeat while failing to meet their nutritional needs.
3. **Diabetes:** A diet high in processed foods, especially those containing refined sugars and high-fructose corn syrup, is a major contributor to the global diabetes epidemic. These foods cause insulin spikes and promote the development of type 2 diabetes.
4. **Cancer:** Certain chemicals found in processed foods, such as artificial sweeteners and preservatives, have been linked to an increased risk of cancer. For example, processed meats contain nitrites and nitrates, which are known to be carcinogenic.
5. **Gut Health:** Processed foods negatively impact the gut microbiome, the community of bacteria that live in our digestive system. These foods can lead to gut inflammation, digestive issues, and even affect the brain, leading to mood disorders.

17.2 A Biblical Perspective on Health and Food

God's Word is filled with wisdom about how we should live in harmony with His creation, and this includes how we treat our bodies. The Bible speaks of health, healing, and the proper relationship between humans and food.

1. **Honor God with Your Body:** The apostle Paul reminds us that our bodies are temples of the Holy Spirit (1 Corinthians 6:19 NIV). Just as we are called to steward the earth, we are also called to care for our own bodies, treating them with respect and gratitude. This includes being mindful of what we eat and how we nourish our bodies.

2. **Diet in Eden:** In the Garden of Eden, God provided Adam and Eve with a plant-based diet (Genesis 1:29 NIV). The fruits of the trees, seeds, and herbs were given for nourishment. This diet was simple, natural, and wholesome, reflecting God's original intention for human health. While the diet after the fall may have changed, God's original design for food offers a blueprint for health.

3. **The Healing Power of Food:** Proverbs 3:7-8 teaches us that wisdom and understanding bring health to the body and nourishment to the bones. In the Bible, food is often associated with healing. Jesus healed the sick by restoring their bodies, and He frequently provided food to the hungry, demonstrating the connection between sustenance and spiritual well-being.

4. **Spiritual and Physical Wholeness:** Jesus not only cared about the spiritual health of those around Him, but He also ministered to their physical needs. He fed the 5,000 (John 6:5-14 NIV), demonstrating that the nourishment of the body is an essential part of our holistic well-being.

17.3 Steps Toward Reclaiming Health

The battle against processed foods and chronic diseases can feel overwhelming, but it is not without hope. There are steps we can take, both individually and collectively, to reclaim our health and restore our bodies. Here are practical and spiritual steps to help you on your journey:

1. **Adopt a Whole Foods Diet:** Begin replacing processed foods with whole, unrefined foods. Focus on vegetables, fruits, whole grains, lean proteins, and healthy fats. These foods provide the nutrients your body needs to function optimally.

2. **Read Labels and Avoid Additives:** Take the time to read the labels on packaged foods. Avoid products that contain artificial additives, preservatives, and excess sugar. The shorter the ingredient list, the better.

3. **Practice Moderation:** While processed foods should be avoided as much as possible, it is important to practice moderation rather than restriction. Allow yourself to enjoy food in balance, and focus on making long-term, sustainable changes to your diet.

4. **Grow Your Own Food:** As we discussed in earlier chapters, growing your own food is one of the most empowering steps you can take. This not only provides you with healthy, fresh produce but also creates a deeper connection to the land and a more intentional approach to nourishment.

5. **Exercise and Rest:** True health involves more than just diet. Engage in regular physical activity, get adequate

sleep, and manage stress. These factors are all interconnected and contribute to overall well-being.

6. **Pray for Healing:** God is the ultimate healer, and we can turn to Him for physical, emotional, and spiritual healing. Prayer for strength, wisdom, and restoration is a key component of reclaiming our health.

17.4 Conclusion: A Call to Restoration

The battle against processed foods and the chronic diseases they cause is not just a fight for physical health; it is a spiritual battle. As we turn back to God's design for food and health, we will not only experience physical healing but also a deeper, more intimate relationship with our Creator.

Chapter 18

The Impact of Processed Foods on Our Families and Communities

As we continue our journey through the modern food crisis, it becomes increasingly clear that the impact of processed foods is not confined to our health alone. The consequences of our modern diet ripple outwards, affecting families, communities, and even entire nations. In this chapter, we will explore how processed foods contribute to the breakdown of the family unit, the erosion of community health, and the consequences for future generations. We will also look at the biblical foundations of community and family health, emphasising the role of stewardship, nurturing relationships, and collective responsibility.

18.1 Processed Foods and Family Health

The family unit is the bedrock of society. It is within the family that children first learn about nutrition, health, and habits that can either promote well-being or contribute to disease. Yet, the increasing reliance on processed foods has profound effects on the physical, emotional, and spiritual health of families.

18.1.1 The Diet of Convenience

In many modern homes, the availability of convenience foods, quick, easy, and often unhealthy, has dramatically changed how families eat. Busy schedules, fast-paced lifestyles, and economic pressures have pushed families toward fast food chains, ready-to-eat meals, and microwaveable snacks. These choices may save time and effort, but they come at a significant cost to health. For children, the foundation of a healthy lifestyle is laid early in life. When children are raised on processed foods, they may develop lifelong habits that lead to obesity, insulin resistance, and even mental health issues. The early introduction of artificial sweeteners, preservatives, and colouring agents can affect children's developing bodies, leading to disrupted metabolism and immune system imbalances. The emotional impact cannot be overstated either. Poor diet has been linked to mood swings, anxiety, and even depression in children and adults alike. When processed foods dominate the family table, families often lose the opportunity to share in the joy of preparing meals together, creating bonds through cooking, and teaching healthy habits.

18.1.2 Spiritual Consequences for Families

In a Christian family, food should not only be seen as nourishment for the body but also as a means of building relationships and deepening spiritual communion. Shared meals are often a reflection of God's love, where families come together in fellowship, gratitude, and joy. When meals are replaced by processed, pre-packaged foods, these spiritual benefits are lost. Instead of a time of nourishment and connection, mealtime becomes a fleeting, disconnected event. In the Bible, meals were a symbol of God's provision and a means of fellowship. Jesus Himself shared meals with His disciples, and the Lord's Supper was a central aspect of Christian community. When families rely heavily on processed foods, they may lose sight of the deeper meaning behind sharing meals and teaching the next generation the importance of gratitude and nourishment from God.

18.2 Processed Foods and Community Health

The consequences of a diet based on processed foods extend far beyond the family unit. They permeate entire communities and contribute to the growing health crisis that many nations are facing. As the consumption of processed foods increases, so does the prevalence of chronic diseases within local populations.

18.2.1 Health Systems Overburdened

As more people fall victim to diet-related diseases such as diabetes, obesity, hypertension, and heart disease, healthcare systems around the world are being overburdened. The costs associated with these chronic conditions, both in terms of medical expenses and lost productivity, are staggering. As treatment becomes more widespread, healthcare services are stretched thin, often focusing on managing symptoms rather than addressing the root causes. The economic burden on families and communities is also severe. The rise in healthcare costs, absenteeism from work, and reduced life expectancy places a heavy toll on the economy. Communities become fractured as members suffer from preventable diseases, and the collective strength of society is diminished.

18.2.2 The Erosion of Traditional Food Cultures

Processed foods are not just harming the health of individuals; they are also eroding traditional food cultures. Communities that once relied on fresh, locally sourced foods and traditional cooking methods are increasingly adopting Western-style diets dominated by fast foods, sugary snacks, and pre-packaged meals. This cultural shift not only threatens nutritional health but also the identity of communities. Food is an important part of culture, and when traditional diets are replaced by processed foods, communities lose part of their heritage. The very act of cooking and sharing meals, once central to community life, is increasingly replaced by convenience and instant gratification, leading to a sense of disconnection and loss of community bonds.

18.3 The Role of Stewardship in Family and Community Health

In Scripture, God calls us to be good stewards of the resources He has given us, which include our bodies, our families, and our communities. Stewardship is about managing well what God has entrusted to us, and it extends beyond the personal to the collective.

18.3.1 Biblical Stewardship of the Body

Our bodies are temples of the Holy Spirit (1 Corinthians 6:19-20 NIV), and as such, we are called to honour God through our care of them. Proper nourishment is an essential part of this stewardship. By rejecting the unhealthy, processed foods that are so prevalent in our modern world, we honour God by treating our bodies with respect and care. For families, this means taking the time to prepare healthy meals together, growing food in our gardens when possible, and teaching children about the importance of making wise food choices. Families that embrace biblical principles of stewardship will build a foundation for long-term health, spiritual growth, and emotional well-being.

18.3.2 Community Stewardship and Accountability

Communities also have a role to play in promoting health and well-being. As a community, we can advocate for healthier food options, support local farmers, and work together to create environments that encourage healthy eating. Churches, schools, and community organisations can play a significant role in educating and empowering people to make better food choices. Communities that work together to reclaim their health also have the potential to bring glory to God through collective action. When a community embraces wholesome living in all areas of life, it becomes a reflection of the health and vibrancy that God desires for His people.

18.4 Rebuilding Health from the Ground Up

Reclaiming the health of our families and communities is a multi-faceted process. It involves personal commitment, collective action, and a return to the values that God has established for human flourishing. Here are several practical steps that can help rebuild health on a family and community level:

1. **Education and Awareness:** The first step is to educate families and communities about the dangers of processed foods. This involves understanding the ingredients, the health risks, and the economic impact of relying on unhealthy food sources. Churches and community centres can host nutrition workshops and cooking classes to empower families to make informed decisions.

2. **Advocating for Change:** Communities can also take collective action to advocate for healthier food environments. This might involve campaigning for access to fresh produce, supporting local farmers' markets, and encouraging schools to provide nutritious meals for children.

3. **Building Stronger Family Traditions:** Rebuilding strong family traditions around food is crucial. Cooking together, growing food in family gardens, and celebrating meals with gratitude and fellowship can bring families closer together and help them cultivate healthier habits.

4. **Promoting Wellness in the Church:** The church has an important role to play in fostering health and well-being. By offering support groups, health ministries, and encouraging a culture of holistic well-being, the church can provide spiritual guidance alongside practical support for families and communities.

18.5 Conclusion: Restoring Our Health, One Family at a Time

The rise of processed foods has not only affected our physical health, but it has also undermined the foundations of our families and communities. Yet, God's call for us to steward our bodies, our families, and our communities remains unchanged. By returning to biblical principles of nourishment, we can reclaim our health and restore the vital relationships that strengthen our families and communities. As we continue this journey toward restoration, let us remember that every step we take toward healthier living is a step toward honouring God with our bodies and our communities. Together, we can rebuild what has been lost and create a future where health and wholeness are the foundation of our families, our churches, and our nations.

Chapter 19

The Global Epidemic of Diet-Related Diseases

The modern food revolution, fuelled by the rise of processed foods, has sparked an unprecedented global epidemic of diet-related diseases. From the bustling streets of New York to the remote villages of Africa, people are suffering from illnesses directly linked to poor eating habits, particularly those involving processed foods. This chapter delves into the extent of the global health crisis, its far-reaching consequences, and the urgent need for a return to biblical principles of health and natural living. We will explore how diseases such as diabetes, heart disease, obesity, and cancer are increasingly prevalent worldwide, particularly in developed and developing nations. We will also look at the economic burden these diseases place on healthcare systems and society at large, and how a change in dietary habits can reverse the trajectory of these illnesses.

19.1 The Rising Tide of Diet-Related Diseases

In the last few decades, we have witnessed an alarming increase in diet-related diseases. While heart disease, stroke, and diabetes have been long-standing health issues, their prevalence is rapidly accelerating in both developed and developing countries. This rise can be traced directly to the widespread consumption of processed foods, laden with sugars, trans fats, and artificial additives.

19.1.1 Obesity and Metabolic Diseases

One of the most visible and concerning outcomes of the processed food epidemic is the rise in obesity. According to the World Health Organization (WHO), global obesity rates have tripled since 1975. This is particularly problematic as obesity is linked to a range of other serious health conditions, such as type 2 diabetes, hypertension, and cardiovascular diseases. The core of the obesity epidemic lies in the consumption of empty calories, foods that are high in sugar and fat but low in nutritional value. Sugary snacks, soft drinks, and fast foods are staples in many diets today, and they contribute significantly to the metabolic dysfunction observed in populations worldwide.

19.1.2 Cardiovascular Diseases

Cardiovascular diseases, including heart disease, stroke, and high blood pressure, have become the leading cause of death globally. These diseases are strongly correlated with poor dietary choices, particularly the overconsumption of saturated fats, trans fats, and refined carbohydrates. Processed foods, which often contain hydrogenated oils and artificial preservatives, promote inflammation, damage blood vessels, and increase the risk of atherosclerosis. The rise of processed food consumption, coupled with a sedentary lifestyle, has led to a public health crisis where an entire generation faces a higher risk of developing heart disease from an early age. This crisis is not only a medical issue but also an economic one, as heart disease treatment and prevention place enormous strain on healthcare systems.

19.1.3 Cancer and the Role of Processed Foods

Processed foods also play a role in the rise of cancer. Studies have linked diets high in processed meats, sugars, and artificial additives to increased risks of various cancers, including colon, breast, and pancreatic cancer. The World Health Organization has classified processed meats as a Group 1 carcinogen, linking them directly to the development of cancer. As the global consumption of processed foods continues to rise, so does the incidence of diet-related cancers, placing a greater burden on public health systems and families alike.

19.2 The Global Economic Burden of Diet-Related Diseases

The rise in diet-related diseases is not only an individual and familial tragedy; it has a massive economic impact as well. As more people are diagnosed with chronic diseases linked to processed foods, the financial strain on healthcare systems worldwide becomes unsustainable.

19.2.1 Healthcare Costs Soar

In both developed and developing countries, the costs associated with treating diseases like diabetes, heart disease, and cancer are skyrocketing. According to a report from the World Economic Forum, the global economic burden of non-communicable diseases (NCDs) is projected to reach $47 trillion by 2030. This is more than the combined GDP of many nations and highlights the urgent need for preventative measures. A significant portion of these healthcare costs stems from the treatment of chronic diseases that are directly linked to poor diets. These diseases not only require expensive long-term care but also lead to early mortality, which further exacerbates the economic strain on societies.

19.2.2 Loss of Productivity

In addition to the direct healthcare costs, there is the issue of lost productivity. Chronic diseases like diabetes and heart disease often result in long-term absenteeism from work, disability, and premature death. These losses reduce the economic output of entire countries and contribute to the increasing wealth gap, especially in low- and middle-income countries. Families and communities bear the brunt of this loss, as individuals affected by chronic diseases face reduced earning potential, impacting the economic stability of households. In many cases, the cost of treating these diseases places families in a cycle of poverty.

19.3 The Globalisation of the Processed Food Crisis

Processed foods are not just a local issue; they have become a global problem. The expansion of multinational food companies and the widespread availability of processed foods have led to a global dietary shift. As Western diets dominated by processed foods spread to other parts of the world, countries with previously healthy traditional diets are seeing a rise in diet-related diseases.

19.3.1 The Western Diet Goes Global

The Western diet, characterised by fast food, high sugar and salt content, and highly processed foods, has spread across the globe, particularly in urban areas. As people in developing countries adopt these dietary habits, they experience a sharp rise in obesity, diabetes, and heart disease. Countries such as China, India, and Mexico have seen dramatic increases in diet-related diseases as Western foods have become more accessible and affordable. This global dietary shift is leading to a rise in non-communicable diseases (NCDs) in countries where infectious diseases were once the primary health concern. The World Health Organization has labelled the global rise in NCDs as one of the most serious public health challenges of the 21st century.

19.3.2 The Impact on Developing Nations

For many developing nations, the adoption of processed foods is often seen as a symbol of progress and modernisation. However, the reality is that these foods come at a great cost to health. Traditional diets, which often include whole grains, vegetables, and lean proteins, are being replaced by cheap processed options high in sugar, salt, and fat. This dietary shift contributes to the rise of obesity and diet-related diseases, putting additional strain on healthcare systems that are already struggling to address the burden of infectious diseases. Moreover, the cost of treatment for chronic diseases in these countries is often prohibitively expensive, making it difficult for families to access the care they need.

19.4 The Biblical Response to Global Health Crisis

The Bible offers a clear framework for addressing issues related to health and well-being. God's original design for food, as seen in the Garden of Eden, emphasises a diet based on whole, natural foods that nourish the body and honour God's creation. The biblical principles of stewardship, balance, and moderation can guide us toward healthier eating habits and more sustainable lifestyles.

19.4.1 Stewardship of the Body

As mentioned in earlier chapters, the Bible teaches that our bodies are temples of the Holy Spirit (1 Corinthians 6:19-20 NIV). This calls us to care for our bodies, not only through physical activity but also through healthy eating. Embracing a biblical diet, one that focuses on fresh fruits, vegetables, whole grains, and lean meats, aligns with the principle of stewardship.

19.4.2 God's Provision of Natural Foods

In Genesis 1:29, God provided plants and fruits as food for mankind. This divine provision points to the wisdom of eating foods that are grown naturally, without the need for processing or the addition of harmful chemicals. A return to this biblical ideal can help heal the global health crisis and restore the health of individuals and communities worldwide.

19.5 Conclusion: Reversing the Crisis Through Change

The global epidemic of diet-related diseases is a serious and growing problem. However, it is not without hope. By returning to healthier eating habits, advocating for whole foods, and embracing biblical principles of stewardship, we can begin to reverse the tide of chronic diseases. The call to return to God's original design for food is a call to healing, both personally and collectively. As we continue this journey, let us be motivated by the understanding that through faith and obedience to God's instructions, we can reclaim our health and restore our communities. Together, we can build a future where health, well-being, and holistic living are the foundation of a global revival.

Chapter 20

Reclaiming the Garden: Returning to God's Design for Food

As we've explored the widespread impact of processed foods and their contribution to global health crises, the modern world is caught in a cycle of deterioration, not only of our bodies but of our entire ecosystem. In this chapter, we will explore the path forward, a return to God's design for food, as described in the Garden of Eden, and how this can lead to both personal and global healing. The principle that God intended food to be nourishing, pure, and life-giving is deeply embedded in scripture, and it stands in stark contrast to the processed and artificial foods we consume today. In this chapter, we will look at how returning to God's original plan can restore our health, protect the environment, and restore our relationship with our Creator.

20.1 The Garden of Eden: A Blueprint for Food and Health

The story of Eden in the Bible presents the ideal diet and lifestyle. In Genesis 1:29, God tells Adam and Eve: *"Behold, I have given you every plant yielding seed that is on the face of all the earth, and every tree with seed in its fruit. You shall have them for food."* This verse outlines God's perfect provision for His creation. In Eden, the diet was simple: fruits, vegetables, and seeds, everything in its natural state, grown in fertile, untouched soil. This was a diet designed to maintain health, vitality, and communion with the Creator. It was a diet that nourished the body and aligned with God's perfect order for the world.

20.1.1 The Purpose of Food: Nourishment and Fellowship

The purpose of food in the Garden was not just sustenance, but also to foster a deeper connection with God. As humans consumed the food God provided, they were not only receiving physical nourishment but were also reflecting God's goodness and provision. Food was a way to partake in the divine order and experience fellowship with God. This principle remains true for us today, when we eat what God has provided in its natural state, we honour both the gift of food and the Creator.

20.1.2 The Dangers of the Fall: The Introduction of Corruption

With the Fall came corruption, not only in the human soul but also in the natural world. As sin entered the world, the very food that was once pure became subject to decay and corruption. In Genesis 3:17-19, God declares the curse on the earth: *"Cursed is the ground because of you; in pain you shall eat of it all the days of your life; thorns and thistles it shall bring forth for you."* This curse affected every aspect of life, including food production. The once-abundant, uncontaminated food that sustained Adam and Eve became subject to toil, thorns, and thistles. This is where the process of degeneration began. Over time, humanity has strayed further from God's original provision, leading to the overprocessing and contamination of food.

20.2 The Modern Diet: A Deviation from Eden's Design

In stark contrast to Eden's simple and wholesome foods, today's modern diet is riddled with refined sugars, preservatives, and artificial ingredients. The introduction of processed foods, combined with industrial agriculture, has led us far away from God's original dietary design. What was once meant to be a source of life has become a source of disease and decay.

20.2.1 The Rise of Processed Foods

The industrial revolution brought with it a wave of innovation, including the mass production of food. While these advances were intended to make food more accessible, they also introduced a system of food manipulation that stripped food of its natural nutrients and added chemicals, artificial flavours, and preservatives. Modern diets now consist of heavily processed items that bear little resemblance to their original, whole-food counterparts. For example, instead of enjoying fresh fruits and vegetables, we often consume sugary snacks, fast food, and frozen dinners. The result is a loss of vitality and an increase in chronic conditions such as obesity, heart disease, and diabetes.

20.2.2 The Loss of Nutritional Value

Many of today's processed foods are designed for convenience and taste, but they come at the expense of nutrition. Whole foods, such as grains, fruits, and vegetables, contain an intricate balance of vitamins, minerals, and antioxidants that support the body's natural healing and defence mechanisms. However, these essential nutrients are often lost in the processing stages. For example, when wheat is refined into white flour, most of the fibre, vitamins, and minerals are removed, leaving behind a product that provides empty calories rather than nourishing sustenance. Similarly, foods that are highly processed often contain unhealthy fats and sugars, which contribute to inflammation and increase the risk of chronic diseases.

20.3 Returning to Eden's Diet: The Path to Healing

While the modern world has strayed far from Eden's design, there is hope. Healing and restoration are possible through a return to the natural, whole foods that God originally provided. This return is not just about dietary change, but about reclaiming a lifestyle that values health, balance, and spiritual connection.

20.3.1 Embracing Whole Foods

A return to whole foods means choosing unprocessed, natural foods, fruits, vegetables, nuts, seeds, and whole grains over processed options. These foods are filled with the nutrients the body needs to thrive, and they nourish the body in the same way God intended in the Garden of Eden. The principle is simple: eat foods as close to their natural form as possible. By doing so, we can avoid the harmful additives and chemicals found in processed foods and restore health to our bodies.

20.3.2 The Importance of Organic and Sustainable Practices

In addition to eating whole foods, it is important to consider how those foods are produced. Organic farming and sustainable agricultural practices promote a holistic approach to food production that respects both the environment and the health of the consumer. These practices focus on growing food without the use of harmful pesticides, chemicals, or genetically modified organisms (GMOs), which can have long-term negative effects on both human health and the ecosystem. As we move towards sustainability, we also begin to recognise the importance of stewardship, not only of our bodies but also of the earth itself. By choosing organic and locally grown foods, we can help support a system that is more in line with God's original design for food and farming.

20.3.3 Spiritual Renewal through Health

Returning to Eden's diet is not just about physical health; it's also about spiritual renewal. The foods we eat have a profound impact on our minds and spirits. In 1 Corinthians 10:31, Paul reminds us: *"So, whether you eat or drink, or whatever you do, do all to the glory of God."* Eating in a way that aligns with God's natural order brings us into deeper fellowship with Him. It is a way to honour God, as we acknowledge that He is the source of all good things and that our bodies are a gift meant to be cared for.

20.4 Conclusion: A Call to Reclaim Our Health

The return to God's original plan for food is not a trend or a passing fad; it is a biblical mandate that calls us to honour God with our bodies and the food we consume. By embracing a diet based on whole, natural foods, we can not only improve our health but also foster a deeper relationship with God and His creation. As we reclaim our health through a return to Eden's design, we are also called to be agents of change in a world struggling with disease and despair. Through the choices we make, individually and collectively, we can help turn the tide of the global health crisis and restore God's kingdom on earth.

Chapter 21

A Global Awakening
Turning the Tide Against Processed Foods

The crisis we are facing today is not merely a product of the modern world's busy lifestyle or the evolving nature of food production; it is a direct result of turning away from God's design. The unprecedented rise of processed foods has led to an epidemic of chronic diseases, environmental degradation, and spiritual disconnection. But there is hope. A global awakening is emerging, and it begins with a simple, yet profound change: the choice to reject the processed and embrace the natural. This chapter will explore how a global movement can shift the tides back to a healthier, more sustainable world, one that aligns with God's original plan for His creation.

21.1 The Global Health Crisis: A Wake-Up Call

The current state of health worldwide is a wake-up call that demands urgent action. Obesity, diabetes, heart disease, and cancer have reached epidemic proportions in nearly every country. According to the World Health Organization (WHO), unhealthy diets are one of the leading causes of death and disability globally. The rise of these diseases coincides directly with the increase in processed food consumption. The connection between the modern diet and the increase in chronic diseases is undeniable. As we have seen in previous chapters, processed foods, filled with refined sugars, artificial preservatives, and toxic chemicals, wreak havoc on the body. This dietary shift has not only led to physical deterioration but also emotional and mental strain. The global burden of disease is compounded by the economic cost of healthcare and the emotional cost borne by individuals and families affected by these health issues.

21.1.1 The Toll on Mental and Emotional Health

The impact of processed foods on mental and emotional health cannot be overstated. Studies have shown that diets high in sugar and artificial additives are linked to higher levels of anxiety, depression, and mood disorders. The chemicals used in processed foods can interfere with brain function, disrupt hormonal balances, and create addictions to sugar and unhealthy fats. This further exacerbates the downward spiral of mental health and physical health, contributing to the global mental health crisis.

21.2 The Environmental Impact: God's Creation in Peril

The shift toward processed foods has not only damaged human health but has also placed a massive strain on the environment. Industrial agriculture, which is responsible for producing the bulk of processed foods, contributes to deforestation, soil depletion, and water contamination. The demand for monoculture crops, such as corn and soybeans, which are primarily grown for processed food production, has led to the destruction of ecosystems and the loss of biodiversity.

21.2.1 The Dangers of Factory Farming

In addition to monoculture farming, the rise of factory farming, where animals are confined to small spaces and fed a diet of unnatural, processed grains, has resulted in animal cruelty and environmental degradation. The excessive use of antibiotics in factory farming has led to the rise of antibiotic-resistant bacteria, which pose a severe threat to human health. Furthermore, factory farms are major contributors to greenhouse gas emissions, further accelerating climate change. The Bible reminds us that God created the earth with an order and purpose, and we are entrusted with the responsibility of being good stewards of His creation. In Genesis 2:15, God places Adam in the Garden of Eden and commands him to work it and take care of it. This responsibility extends beyond our own health; it encompasses the well-being of the earth and all living creatures.

21.2.2 Restoring the Land: Sustainable Practices

A return to God's original design for food also involves a commitment to sustainable agriculture. Practices such as organic farming, regenerative agriculture, and permaculture emphasise the restoration of soil health, biodiversity, and natural ecosystems. These practices are rooted in a biblical understanding of stewardship and can significantly reduce the environmental impact of food production.

21.3 The Role of Education: Spreading the Truth

One of the most powerful tools in the global fight against processed foods is education. People must understand the health risks associated with modern diets and the impact of processed foods on their bodies, minds, and the environment. As Christians, we are called to speak truth in love and to raise awareness of how we can care for our bodies as temples of the Holy Spirit (1 Corinthians 6:19-20 NIV).

21.3.1 Raising Awareness in Communities

A key part of this educational movement is raising awareness in local communities about the dangers of processed foods. From churches to schools to local health organisations, it is crucial to educate people about the benefits of a whole-food diet and the biblical perspective on food. This can be achieved through workshops, seminars, and outreach programs that focus on providing knowledge about healthier alternatives to processed foods.

21.3.2 The Power of Media and Social Platforms

In addition to grassroots education, the media plays an essential role in shaping public opinion. Social media platforms, documentaries, and books that focus on the dangers of processed foods and the benefits of whole foods can reach a wide audience. A shift in public perception is necessary to create a demand for more natural, sustainable food options.

21.4 The Global Movement: A Call to Action

The global movement to reclaim our health and environment requires a unified effort from individuals, communities, governments, and industries. Each person can make a difference by choosing to eat whole, natural foods and advocating for sustainable practices.

21.4.1 The Role of the Church

The Church has a critical role to play in this global awakening. Christians are called to be agents of transformation in the world, and this includes taking a stand against the destructive practices of industrial food production. By promoting healthy eating and environmental stewardship, the Church can lead the way in showing the world a better, more sustainable way to live. The Bible speaks of our responsibility to care for both our bodies and God's creation. In doing so, we can honour God and create a better future for generations to come.

21.4.2 Advocacy for Change in Policy

In addition to personal responsibility, we must also advocate for policy changes that promote healthier food systems. Governments should implement policies that support organic farming, food labelling, and regulations on the use of harmful chemicals and preservatives. Advocacy efforts at the local, national, and international levels can help create the political will needed to change the food industry's focus from profit-driven motives to human and environmental well-being.

21.5 Conclusion: A New Beginning

The global crisis we face today, driven by the consumption of processed foods, is a call to action. We have strayed far from the original plan that God set for us in the Garden of Eden, but it is not too late to return. By reclaiming the simplicity and purity of the foods God designed for us, we can restore our health, our communities, and our environment. It is time for a global awakening, a return to natural, life-giving foods that honour God and His creation.

Chapter 22

The Return to Eden
Reclaiming the Divine Diet

In Genesis 1:29 NIV, God gave mankind a blueprint for what we were to eat: "And God said, 'Behold, I have given you every herb bearing seed, which is upon the face of all the earth, and every tree, in the which is the fruit of a tree yielding seed; to you it shall be for meat.'" This was God's original dietary plan for humanity: whole, natural, plant-based food, free from the processed chemicals and artificial additives that now dominate modern diets. The wisdom embedded in God's creation speaks to the profound relationship between the spiritual, physical, and environmental well-being of humanity. This chapter will explore how returning to the Edenic diet is not just a way to reclaim our health, but also to restore our relationship with God and His creation.

22.1 The Genesis Diet: A Blueprint for Life

When God created the world, He designed a harmonious relationship between mankind and the earth. In the Garden of Eden, the diet given to humanity was one of abundance and purity: fruits, vegetables, seeds, and nuts. These were the foods that nourished Adam and Eve, providing everything their bodies needed for optimal health and vitality. There was no mention of processed food or animal products in the Edenic diet, which suggests that God's original plan was centred on whole plant foods. The diet described in Genesis 1:29 NIV was also free from the harmful additives, preservatives, and chemical treatments that have come to dominate modern food systems. The perfection of God's creation is evident in the nutrition found in the earth's natural resources, and this diet is what humans were designed to thrive on.

22.1.1 Spiritual and Physical Health Intertwined

The Edenic diet wasn't just about physical health; it was also about maintaining a spiritual connection with God. The foods we consume have a profound impact on our mental and emotional well-being, and this connection has been lost in the pursuit of convenience and artificial enhancements. By returning to the natural foods designed by God, we not only improve our physical health but also bring ourselves into greater spiritual alignment with His original purpose for us. The foods of Eden were life-giving, offering a deep connection to the Creator through every bite. As we consume whole, natural foods, we can view them as a reflection of God's provision and care, turning every meal into an act of worship and gratitude.

22.2 The Dangers of Departure: The Rise of Processed Foods

The shift away from the Edenic diet began thousands of years ago, but it reached its peak in the modern world with the advent of industrialised agriculture and processed foods. The rise of processed foods has been devastating to our health, the environment, and our relationship with God's creation.

22.2.1 The Deception of Convenience

Processed foods, while convenient, are typically stripped of nutrients and packed with artificial ingredients that disrupt the body's natural processes. Over time, the consumption of these foods has led to a decline in health and an increase in chronic diseases such as obesity, diabetes, and heart disease. The desire for convenience in modern life has led to the abandonment of God's design for nourishment. The manufactured foods of today are detached from the earth's original gifts. They often lack the life-giving nutrients found in natural, whole foods, and instead, contain chemicals, preservatives, and additives that do not serve the body well.

22.3 Returning to Eden: Restoring the Divine Diet

A return to the Edenic diet requires more than just a change in what we eat; it requires a shift in our mindset and a renewed understanding of our role as stewards of God's creation. This shift is about more than personal health; it's about aligning ourselves with God's original purpose for humanity and the world He created.

22.3.1 Rediscovering Whole, Natural Foods

To restore the Edenic diet, we must focus on whole, unprocessed foods that nourish the body in their natural form. This includes:

- **Fruits:** Rich in vitamins, antioxidants, and fibre, fruits are a vital part of the Edenic diet. They are life-giving and provide natural sweetness without the added sugars and preservatives found in processed snacks.
- **Vegetables:** Full of essential nutrients, vegetables are the cornerstone of a healthy diet. They provide the necessary minerals, vitamins, and fibre that support digestion, immunity, and overall health.
- **Nuts and Seeds:** Packed with healthy fats, proteins, and micronutrients, nuts and seeds are perfect additions to a diet based on whole foods. They offer a satisfying and nutritious source of energy.
- **Whole Grains:** Unlike processed grains, whole grains contain all parts of the seed and retain the full range of nutrients, including fibre, B vitamins, and minerals.

22.3.2 Restoring the Land: Regenerative Agriculture

A key component of returning to Eden is restoring the land that has been damaged by industrial farming practices. Regenerative agriculture, which emphasises sustainable and eco-friendly farming methods, is the path to a healthier, more sustainable future. By utilising techniques such as crop rotation, composting, and no-till farming, we can restore the soil, enhance biodiversity, and ensure that the earth continues to provide for future generations.

22.4 The Role of the Church: Leading the Way

As believers, we have a moral obligation to care for our bodies and the world God created. The Church can play a pivotal role in leading a global movement back to the Edenic diet by promoting education, awareness, and action. This can be done through:

- Biblical teaching on the importance of health and stewardship of God's creation.
- Hosting workshops on healthy eating and sustainable farming practices.
- Advocating for policy changes that support organic farming and the reduction of processed foods in the marketplace.

By integrating these principles into our churches and communities, we can create a movement that not only changes the way we eat but also helps restore the relationship between humanity, creation, and the Creator.

22.5 Conclusion: A Divine Reset

The return to the Edenic diet is not just a health trend; it is a spiritual journey back to the heart of God's plan for His creation. By choosing whole, natural foods and embracing sustainable farming practices, we can reclaim the vitality and spiritual connection that God originally intended for us. In returning to Eden, we acknowledge that the food we eat is not just for our physical bodies; it is a means of worship and gratitude for God's provision. As we nourish our bodies with the foods God designed for us, we also restore our relationship with Him and His creation. It is time to make a conscious choice to return to Eden, honouring both our health and the earth He entrusted to us.

Chapter 23

The Global Impact
Processed Food and the Modern World

In the modern world, processed foods have become a global epidemic, contributing to the rise of chronic diseases, obesity, and malnutrition. The spread of these artificial food systems is not just an individual health crisis; it's a worldwide issue, deeply affecting economies, environments, and societies. This chapter explores the global impact of processed foods, how they have shaped our world, and what can be done to reverse their devastating effects.

23.1 The Global Shift: From Natural to Processed

The shift from natural, whole foods to processed alternatives has occurred over the past century, driven largely by industrialisation and the rise of mass production. As technologies advanced, food manufacturers sought to increase profits by creating inexpensive, shelf-stable products that could be shipped globally. This revolution in food production came at the expense of the nutritional value and sustainability of what we eat.

23.1.1 A Worldwide Phenomenon

The introduction of processed foods has been widespread, impacting developed and developing nations alike. What began in the West as a convenient and cheap solution for feeding growing populations has now spread to nearly every corner of the globe. The globalisation of processed food has led to significant changes in dietary patterns, particularly in countries where traditional, plant-based diets once dominated. While processed food consumption is highest in wealthier nations, its reach extends to poorer countries as well. The marketing power of multinational food companies has turned processed snacks, sugary beverages, and fast food into global staples, pushing traditional diets aside in favour of cheaper, more accessible alternatives.

23.2 The Health Crisis: Obesity, Disease, and Malnutrition

The consumption of processed foods is one of the leading contributors to the global health crisis. These foods are often high in sugars, unhealthy fats, sodium, and refined grains, which are linked to a wide range of diseases. The health consequences are far-reaching, with obesity, heart disease, diabetes, and hypertension becoming increasingly prevalent in nations around the world.

23.2.1 Obesity: A Global Pandemic

Obesity has reached epidemic proportions worldwide. According to the World Health Organization (WHO), more than 1.9 billion adults are overweight, with 650 million of them classified as obese. The rise in obesity rates is directly correlated with the consumption of processed foods, which are typically calorie-dense but nutrient-poor. What makes processed foods particularly dangerous is their ability to create food dependency. High in added sugars and fats, they trigger the brain's reward system, leading to overconsumption. This cycle of addiction is contributing to rising rates of obesity and related diseases across the globe.

23.2.2 Chronic Diseases and Non-Communicable Diseases (NCDs)

Processed food consumption is also linked to the rise of chronic diseases, conditions that last a year or more and require ongoing medical attention. Diseases such as type 2 diabetes, cardiovascular disease, and certain cancers are now among the leading causes of death worldwide. These diseases are often preventable, yet their connection to diet and lifestyle is often ignored or downplayed in favour of pharmaceutical solutions. One of the largest contributors to these diseases is the high intake of processed sugars and trans fats, both of which are prevalent in many packaged and fast foods. Trans fats are known to raise levels of bad cholesterol (LDL) while lowering levels of good cholesterol (HDL), increasing the risk of heart disease.

23.3 The Environmental Cost: Processed Foods and the Planet

The rise of processed foods has also placed a significant burden on the environment. The industrialisation of food production has led to unsustainable farming practices, overuse of resources, and increased pollution, contributing to the global climate crisis.

23.3.1 Unsustainable Farming Practices

The mass production of processed foods requires vast amounts of raw materials, including grains, sugar, meat, and vegetable oils. These ingredients are often produced using monoculture farming, a method that depletes soil health, increases pesticide use, and contributes to environmental degradation. In addition, the livestock industry, which is closely tied to processed food production, is a major source of greenhouse gas emissions, deforestation, and water consumption. Factory farming, which supplies the meat for processed foods, has led to significant environmental destruction, including the loss of biodiversity and damage to ecosystems.

23.3.2 Food Waste: The Impact of Overproduction

Another environmental cost of processed foods is the amount of food waste generated. The rise of mass-produced, pre-packaged food often results in items being discarded due to overproduction, spoilage, and packaging waste. According to the Food and Agriculture Organization (FAO), one-third of all food produced is lost or wasted each year, contributing to unnecessary environmental damage.

23.4 Economic Consequences: The Cost of Processed Foods

The economic consequences of processed food consumption are multifaceted. While processed foods may seem inexpensive at the point of purchase, the hidden costs are immense. These costs are seen in the healthcare system, the environment, and the global economy as a whole.

23.4.1 Healthcare Costs

The health consequences of processed food consumption place a tremendous strain on healthcare systems worldwide. Treating obesity, diabetes, heart disease, and other chronic conditions associated with poor diets is a multibillion-dollar endeavour. According to the Centres for Disease Control and Prevention (CDC), the total cost of obesity in the United States alone was $147 billion in 2008. As the global obesity epidemic continues to grow, healthcare costs will rise accordingly.

23.4.2 Economic Inequality and Food Access

Processed foods are often cheaper and more accessible than healthy alternatives, making them more appealing to low-income populations. However, this accessibility comes with a long-term cost. By investing in processed foods instead of whole, nutrient-dense options, individuals may be saving money upfront, but they will pay for it later in healthcare expenses and lost productivity.

23.5 Solutions: Reversing the Trend

The global rise of processed foods is a massive challenge, but it is not insurmountable. Reversing the negative effects of processed foods requires a global shift in diet, policy, and agriculture.

23.5.1 Promoting Whole Foods and Sustainable Agriculture

To combat the rise of processed foods, nations must promote policies that support whole food systems, including local, organic farming, and regenerative agriculture. Encouraging people to return to plant-based, whole foods is the first step in reversing the damage done by processed foods.

23.5.2 Global Awareness and Education

Awareness campaigns must be launched to educate consumers about the dangers of processed foods and the benefits of whole, natural diets. This education should focus on the long-term health benefits of a whole food diet, as well as the environmental impact of industrial food systems.

23.5.3 The Role of Governments and Policy

Governments can help by imposing regulations on food labelling, ensuring that processed foods are clearly marked with nutritional information. Policies that encourage healthier food choices, such as subsidies for fresh produce and taxes on sugary beverages, can also play a significant role in improving global health.

23.6 Conclusion: A Global Call to Action

The global impact of processed foods is undeniable. The damage to our health, environment, and economies is vast, but it is not too late to make a change. By returning to whole, natural foods and promoting sustainable food systems, we can reverse the damage and create a healthier, more sustainable future for all. The challenge lies in the willingness of individuals, communities, and governments to embrace this shift toward healthier, sustainable living. The call to action is clear: we must choose wisely, not just for our own health, but for the well-being of the entire planet.

Chapter 24

The Biblical Perspective
Return to Eden's Food Plan

Throughout history, the human race has often looked to God's Word for wisdom and guidance. In the story of creation, we are given a model for living that includes not only how we should live but also what we should eat. In Genesis, God provided a diet designed to sustain and nourish humanity. However, humanity's shift away from God's original design has led to devastating consequences, particularly through the consumption of processed foods. This chapter examines Eden's original food plan, the wisdom behind God's dietary guidelines, and how the modern world's embrace of processed foods contrasts sharply with the divine model. The return to Eden's plan is more than a spiritual or theological notion; it has profound implications for our health, our environment, and our relationship with the Creator.

24.1 Eden's Original Diet: A Blueprint for Health

In Genesis 1:29, God's first directive regarding food was clear: *"And God said, 'Behold, I have given you every herb bearing seed, which is upon the face of all the earth, and every tree, in the which is the fruit of a tree yielding seed; to you it shall be for meat.'"* (KJV). This verse highlights the plant-based diet that was designed for humanity's nourishment. God's initial plan was for humans to consume fruits, seeds, and vegetables, which are inherently packed with the nutrients, fibres, and vitamins necessary for long-term health and vitality. God's design was intentional; food in its whole, natural form was meant to be the perfect fuel for the human body.

24.2 The Wisdom of Whole Foods

God's original food plan was whole, unrefined, and free from artificial additives. It was perfect for the body's needs. Fruits, vegetables, grains, and seeds provide the ideal balance of carbohydrates, proteins, fats, vitamins, and minerals required for health. They support immune function, digestion, and cellular repair while minimising the negative health effects often caused by modern diets. God's choice of foods is also a lesson in divine wisdom. The natural foods He created are unprocessed, sustainable, and pure. They have the power to provide long-term health because they come directly from the earth, unaltered by human hands. The closer we are to God's original design, the more our health and well-being are aligned with His intentions.

24.3 The Fall: The Introduction of Processed Food

The story of the fall in Genesis 3 marks the tragic departure from God's perfect design. When Adam and Eve ate from the forbidden tree, they chose to take control of their destiny, which led to the introduction of sin, disease, and death into the world. Similarly, the introduction of processed foods into the human diet represents a metaphorical "fall" from the divine design of whole foods. While processed foods may seem convenient, they carry with them the hidden costs of health degradation, addiction, and chronic diseases. These foods are not in line with the sustaining wisdom of Eden's original plan. Like the fruit from the tree of knowledge, they often come with the illusion of satisfaction but deliver long-term harm.

24.3.1 The Illusion of Convenience

Just as Eve saw the forbidden fruit as "good for food" (Genesis 3:6 NIV), modern society has embraced processed foods, which are marketed as being "quick" and "convenient." However, this "convenience" often comes with hidden costs, like the loss of nutrients, overuse of chemicals, and the introduction of ingredients that are difficult for the body to process. What appears easy on the surface can lead to severe health consequences down the line.

24.4 A Call Back to Eden: Restoring God's Food Plan

To heal the world's health crises, a return to the principles established in Eden is essential. A restoration of God's original food plan is not just about eating "better," it's about aligning our food choices with God's purposes for humanity. This requires a fundamental shift in the way we view food, health, and our relationship with creation.

24.4.1 Rediscovering Whole Foods

Returning to whole foods, much like the fruits, seeds, and grains from the Garden of Eden, is not a call for asceticism but a return to a divine blueprint for health. By embracing more plant-based foods, organic produce, and unrefined grains, we can restore vitality to our bodies. God's design for us was one of health, wholeness, and sustenance, and we are called to steward our bodies and the earth in alignment with this plan.

24.4.2 Ethical and Sustainable Choices

Beyond health, Eden's food plan offers insight into how we should engage with the earth. God created a world where every tree and every seed had a purpose in sustaining life. In the modern context, this means choosing sustainable and ethically sourced foods that honour God's creation and promote the well-being of the planet. This includes reducing the reliance on factory-farming methods, overconsumption of resources, and embracing ethical agricultural practices.

24.5 The Spiritual Connection: Food as Worship

Eating is not just a biological function; it is a spiritual act. In the biblical worldview, food is a gift from God meant to sustain us both physically and spiritually. How we choose to nourish our bodies is also an act of worship, reflecting our relationship with God and His creation. In 1 Corinthians

10:31, Paul writes, *"So, whether you eat or drink, or whatever you do, do it all for the glory of God."* (NIV). By returning to Eden's food plan, we honour God's original design for humanity. Eating whole, unprocessed foods is a form of worship, a conscious act of gratitude and respect for God's provision. Every meal becomes an opportunity to praise the Creator and acknowledge His sovereignty over all aspects of life, including our health.

24.6 The Healing Power of God's Diet: A Call to Action

The world's modern health crisis is rooted in the departure from God's original food plan. But just as God provided the tree of life in the Garden of Eden to restore eternal life (Genesis 2:9 NIV), so too does He offer a way of life through whole, natural foods that can heal and sustain us today. The call is simple: to return to the garden, to choose foods that align with God's design, and to honour Him through the nourishment we give to our bodies. In doing so, we can reverse the damage caused by processed foods. We can heal our bodies, restore our communities, and protect the planet. As stewards of the earth, we are called to care for both the land and our bodies. This is not a new doctrine, but a return to the wisdom of Eden, where the food we eat nourishes us in every way.

24.7 Conclusion: A New Beginning

A return to Eden's food plan is a spiritual, physical, and environmental imperative. It calls us to make choices that honour God's original design, a design that fosters health, wholeness, and sustainability. It challenges us to reject the processed foods that contribute to the global health crisis and embrace the goodness of God's creation. As we move forward, we must reclaim the wisdom found in Genesis and reframe the way we look at food. Through this return, we can experience true healing, physically, emotionally, and spiritually, as we nourish our bodies in accordance with the Creator's plan.

Chapter 25

The Toxic Effects of Processed Foods on the Body

In the modern world, the consumption of processed foods has become so normalised that many people fail to recognise the severe toll they take on the human body. From heart disease to obesity, type 2 diabetes, and digestive disorders, the toxic effects of processed foods are devastating our health. These foods, which often contain high levels of sugar, salt, artificial additives, and trans fats, disrupt the body's natural systems and contribute to a wide range of chronic illnesses. This chapter will explore the chemical and nutritional properties of processed foods, their impact on the human body, and why they are a significant factor in the ongoing global health crisis. We will also look at how the consumption of these foods represents a departure from God's intended design for our health and well-being.

25.1 The Processed Food Industry: A Threat to Health

The processed food industry is a multi-billion-dollar global enterprise that profits from selling foods designed for convenience, taste, and long shelf life, not for optimal health. These foods are often stripped of their natural nutrients and replaced with artificial additives, preservatives, and sugar to enhance flavour and extend shelf life. The ingredients in these products are frequently difficult for the body to recognise and metabolise, leading to a host of negative health consequences. Many processed foods are designed to be hyper-palatable; they are created to be so delicious that they trigger overconsumption. This leads to addiction-like behaviours where the body becomes dependent on the constant influx of sugar, salt, and fat. The result is a rise in obesity and related diseases that are directly linked to processed food consumption.

25.2 The Hidden Dangers of Processed Ingredients

Processed foods are often packed with artificial ingredients that are not naturally found in whole foods. These chemicals, preservatives, and artificial flavours not only contribute to the depletion of the nutritional value of food but also have harmful effects on the body. Let's take a look at some of the most common culprits in processed foods:

25.2.1 Added Sugars and Sweeteners

Sugar has become one of the biggest culprits in the modern diet. While sugar is found naturally in many whole foods, such as fruits, the refined sugars added to processed foods wreak havoc on our health. Excessive sugar consumption has been linked to insulin resistance, inflammation, and fat accumulation, all of which contribute to type 2 diabetes, cardiovascular diseases, and obesity. Furthermore, the artificial sweeteners often used in processed foods may not be as harmless as they seem. Substitutes like aspartame and sucralose have been linked to increased appetite, gut microbiome disruption, and even cancer in some studies. These sweeteners confuse the body's natural hunger cues and increase cravings for sugary foods.

25.2.2 Trans Fats

Once widely used in processed foods due to their low cost and long shelf life, trans fats are now known to be extremely harmful. These fats are created through a process called hydrogenation, which turns liquid oils into solids. Trans fats are linked to a variety of serious health issues, including heart disease, stroke, and diabetes. They raise bad cholesterol (LDL) levels and lower good cholesterol (HDL), disrupting the body's ability to regulate blood fat levels and leading to long-term cardiovascular damage.

25.2.3 Preservatives and Additives

Many processed foods contain preservatives such as BHA, BHT, and propyl gallate, which extend shelf life but may pose health risks. These chemicals have been linked to cancer, hormonal disruption, and allergic reactions. Moreover, food additives like monosodium glutamate (MSG), which is often used to enhance flavour, can cause headaches, nausea, and obesity.

25.3 The Metabolic and Hormonal Disruption Caused by Processed Foods

When processed foods enter the body, they are often broken down into simple sugars and fats, which are absorbed rapidly into the bloodstream. This spikes blood sugar levels, leading to a rapid release of insulin to help regulate those levels. Over time, the body becomes less responsive to insulin, leading to insulin resistance and eventually type 2 diabetes. Moreover, processed foods have been shown to disrupt the body's hormonal balance, particularly regarding leptin and ghrelin, hormones responsible for regulating hunger and satiety. When these hormones are out of balance, it can lead to overeating, weight gain, and a constant feeling of hunger, even after eating. This hormonal disruption is one of the key factors behind the obesity epidemic.

25.4 The Impact on Gut Health: A Forgotten Connection

In recent years, gut health has gained significant attention, as science continues to uncover the critical role that the microbiome plays in overall health. The gut is home to trillions of bacteria, fungi, and other microorganisms that help digest food, produce essential vitamins, and regulate the immune system. Processed foods, particularly those high in refined carbohydrates, artificial sweeteners, and preservatives, can have a devastating effect on the gut microbiome. These foods alter the composition of gut bacteria, decreasing the number of beneficial bacteria and promoting the growth of harmful bacteria. This imbalance, known as dysbiosis, is linked to a variety of chronic conditions, including irritable bowel syndrome (IBS), autoimmune diseases, mental health disorders, and inflammatory diseases.

25.5 Long-Term Consequences: Chronic Diseases and Early Mortality

The long-term effects of a diet high in processed foods are nothing short of catastrophic. As the body accumulates toxic substances, the risk for chronic diseases increases exponentially. Here are just a few of the diseases that are directly associated with processed food consumption:

- **Heart Disease:** High levels of trans fats, added sugars, and salt contribute to the development of atherosclerosis, or the hardening of the arteries, which is a leading cause of heart disease.
- **Obesity and Diabetes:** The high caloric content and poor nutritional value of processed foods are major contributors to the global rise in obesity and type 2 diabetes.
- **Cancer:** Certain chemicals used in processed foods, including preservatives and artificial flavours, have been linked to an increased risk of cancer, particularly breast and colon cancer.
- **Mental Health Disorders:** Studies have shown that a poor diet, especially one rich in processed foods, is associated with a higher incidence of depression, anxiety, and cognitive decline.

25.6 A Call to Action: Returning to Whole Foods

The damage caused by processed foods is undeniable. The global rise in chronic illnesses, from heart disease to cancer, is a direct result of the modern reliance on processed, unhealthy food. Yet there is hope. A return to the original whole foods that God designed for our nourishment is the key to healing the body. By embracing whole, unprocessed foods, fruits, vegetables, grains, legumes, and nuts, we can reverse many of the health problems caused by processed foods. Additionally, choosing organic, ethically sourced food and minimising chemical additives will help restore balance to our bodies and our environment.

25.7 Conclusion: The Healing Power of Returning to Eden's Diet

In conclusion, processed foods represent a departure from God's divine plan for our health. Their harmful effects on the body are evident, and the time has come for us to reject these toxic substances and return to God's original food design. By embracing the whole foods He created, we can restore our bodies to health and begin the process of healing. A return to Eden's diet is not merely a dietary change, it is a spiritual and physical restoration. Just as God provided nourishment in the Garden of Eden, He continues to offer healing through the foods He created for our well-being.

Chapter 26

The Spiritual Connection to Food and Health

In the Bible, food is not just a means of physical sustenance; it is a spiritual tool meant to deepen our relationship with God. From the Garden of Eden, where Adam and Eve were given fruits and plants for nourishment, to the Last Supper, where Jesus shared bread and wine with His disciples, food plays a profound role in God's covenant with His people. In this chapter, we will explore the spiritual significance of food, the connection between health and holiness, and how returning to God's original design for food can lead to both physical and spiritual restoration.

26.1 Food as a Gift from God

The Bible begins with a clear message: food is a gift from God. In the book of Genesis, we see that after creating the earth, God provided mankind with an abundant array of food in the Garden of Eden: "And God said, 'Behold, I have given you every herb bearing seed, which is upon the face of all the earth, and every tree, in which is the fruit of a tree yielding seed; to you it shall be for meat.'" (Genesis 1:29, KJV). From the very beginning, God's design for food was rooted in nourishment, abundance, and divine provision. The fruits, vegetables, and seeds in the Garden of Eden were not just for physical health, but for spiritual communion with God. Eating in Eden was a holistic experience, where body, mind, and spirit were aligned with God's perfect will.

26.2 The Fall and the Disruption of God's Design

When Adam and Eve sinned, their disobedience disrupted not only their relationship with God but also the perfect design for their health and nourishment. The consequences of their sin brought about a shift in the natural world. The abundance they enjoyed in Eden was replaced by toil and suffering, and food became associated with both blessing and curse. "Cursed is the ground for your sake; in sorrow shalt thou eat of it all the days of thy life." (Genesis 3:17, KJV). This curse marked a departure from God's intended design for food, as mankind was now subjected to harsh conditions that would affect their ability to cultivate and enjoy the foods God had originally provided. With the fall came disorder in every area of life, including food.

26.3 Jesus and the Redemptive Power of Food

As we journey through the Old Testament, we see that food continues to be a central theme in God's relationship with His people. The Israelites were given dietary laws, and the feasts and sacrifices provided a means of atonement and worship. But it wasn't until the coming of Jesus Christ that the true redemptive power of food was revealed. Jesus, as the Bread of

Life, took food and used it as a symbol of the kingdom of God and the new covenant between God and humanity. In the Gospel of John, Jesus speaks about the spiritual nourishment He offers: "I am the bread of life: he that cometh to me shall never hunger; and he that believeth on me shall never thirst." (John 6:35, KJV). In the Last Supper, Jesus broke bread with His disciples, symbolising His body that would be broken for them, and He poured wine, symbolising His blood that would be shed for the forgiveness of sins. Through this act, Jesus not only instituted the Eucharist but also redefined food as spiritual sustenance, a means by which believers would continue to partake in the redemptive work of Christ.

26.4 The Body as a Temple

The New Testament emphasises that the body is a temple of the Holy Spirit, and as such, it is our responsibility to honour God with our bodies, including the way we care for them through our diet. Paul writes to the Corinthians: "Know ye not that your body is the temple of the Holy Ghost, which is in you, which ye have of God, and ye are not your own?" (1 Corinthians 6:19, KJV). Just as the Israelites were commanded to maintain purity and holiness in their worship, Christians are called to live in a way that reflects the sanctity of the body. This means that our choices about food are not just about physical health; they are deeply connected to our spiritual health. Eating processed, toxic foods that harm the body is not in alignment with God's plan for us to be healthy, vibrant vessels for His Holy Spirit.

26.5 The Spiritual Significance of Eating Whole, Natural Foods

Eating foods that God has created, fruits, vegetables, grains, and clean meats, brings us back to the original design for nourishment. Whole foods are not only good for the body; they are spiritually significant because they connect us to the Creator. When we consume the food He provided, we acknowledge His provision and give thanks for His abundant blessings. In the Book of Psalms, we see that eating and drinking are acts of worship and gratitude: "The earth is the Lord's, and the fullness thereof; the world, and they that dwell therein." (Psalm 24:1, KJV). By choosing whole foods over processed alternatives, we participate in God's redemptive work, aligning our physical choices with His eternal purposes.

26.6 The Call to Renew Our Diets: A Holistic Approach

The invitation to return to God's original dietary design is not just about improving physical health; it is about restoring our relationship with God. A holistic approach to food, one that includes physical, emotional, and spiritual well-being, reflects our desire to honour God in every aspect of our lives. As we become more mindful of the foods we eat, we also become more aware of God's presence in our lives. This is not just about rejecting processed foods; it is about embracing a lifestyle that prioritises health, holiness, and worship. By eating whole, natural foods, we align ourselves with the divine purpose for our bodies and honour God as the ultimate provider.

26.7 Conclusion: Food as a Path to Spiritual Health

Food is more than just fuel for the body; it is a spiritual act that connects us to God's divine plan. Just as in the Garden of Eden, food was meant to sustain us physically and spiritually. By returning to the whole foods that God designed for our nourishment, we can experience a profound restoration of both body and soul. In embracing this biblical diet, we reclaim God's original plan for our lives and honour Him with our bodies. As we nourish ourselves with the food He provided, we also deepen our relationship with Him and partake in the redemptive work of Christ, who is the true Bread of Life.

Chapter 27

The Impact of Processed Foods on Modern Health

Processed foods are one of the greatest threats to modern health, both physically and spiritually, despite the abundance of easily accessible food. The foods we consume today are often highly processed, filled with chemicals, additives, and artificial ingredients that strip away the nutrients essential for our well-being. This chapter explores the detrimental effects of processed foods on human health, the body's natural systems, and how these modern eating habits align with the global genocide being waged on humanity through poor dietary choices.

27.1 The Rise of Processed Foods

The rise of processed foods in the 20th and 21st centuries is one of the most significant transformations in the global food system. The industrialisation of food production has led to the mass production of food that is convenient, inexpensive, and widely available. However, this convenience comes at a cost: nutritional deficiency, toxicity, and the destruction of the body's natural functions. Historically, our ancestors ate fresh, whole foods that were grown, hunted, or gathered locally. These foods were rich in nutrients, free of artificial preservatives, and aligned with God's design for nourishment. But the advent of modern food processing technologies, such as refining, additives, and artificial flavourings, has created foods that are stripped of their natural benefits and are often harmful to the body.

27.2 Understanding Processed Foods: What Are They?

Processed foods are foods that have been altered from their natural state through methods such as canning, freezing, drying, refining, or the addition of preservatives, colouring, and artificial flavourings. These methods were initially developed to extend shelf life and enhance convenience, but they come at the expense of the food's original nutritional value. Examples of highly processed foods include:

- Fast food (burgers, fries, and pizza)
- Snack foods (chips, cookies, and candy)
- Sugary drinks (soda, energy drinks, and sweetened beverages)
- Packaged meals (instant noodles, frozen dinners)
- Refined grains (white bread, white rice, and pasta)
- Processed meats (hot dogs, sausages, and deli meats)

These foods are often low in fibre, vitamins, and minerals, while being high in sugars, unhealthy fats, and sodium. The consumption of such foods over time leads to chronic diseases, including obesity, heart disease, diabetes, and even cancer.

27.3 The Body's Response to Processed Foods

The human body was designed to function on whole, natural foods. When we consume highly processed foods, the body struggles to process the artificial ingredients and toxic additives. Over time, these foods can wreak havoc on our body's systems, including the digestive system, immune system, and hormonal balance.

27.3.1 Nutrient Depletion

Processed foods are often void of essential nutrients. For example, the refining process of grains strips away most of the fibre, vitamins, and minerals found in the whole grain. This leads to nutrient deficiencies, which can cause a range of health problems, such as fatigue, weakened immune function, and cognitive decline.

27.3.2 Toxicity and Chemical Load

Many processed foods contain chemicals that are harmful to the body. These chemicals include artificial preservatives, colourings, and flavour enhancers, such as monosodium glutamate (MSG) and aspartame, which have been linked to neurological damage and other health concerns. Over time, the chemical load from processed foods can overwhelm the liver and kidneys, leading to chronic health issues, such as liver disease, kidney stones, and an increased cancer risk.

27.3.3 Hormonal Disruption

Processed foods are also often high in refined sugars and trans fats, both of which disrupt the body's hormonal balance. High sugar intake can lead to insulin resistance, a precursor to Type 2 diabetes, while trans fats can affect the body's ability to regulate cholesterol levels, contributing to heart disease. Furthermore, many processed foods contain endocrine-disrupting chemicals that interfere with hormone production and function.

27.4 The Global Impact: Health Crisis and Economic Burden

The global consumption of processed foods has led to an epidemic of diet-related diseases. According to the World Health Organization (WHO), non-communicable diseases (NCDs) such as heart disease, diabetes, and cancer account for more than 70% of global deaths. A significant contributor to this crisis is the Western diet, characterised by high consumption of processed foods, sugar, and refined grains. The economic burden of these diseases is staggering. The cost of treating chronic conditions linked to poor diet is estimated to be in the trillions of dollars annually, straining healthcare systems worldwide. Yet, despite the overwhelming evidence of the harm caused by processed foods, they continue to be heavily marketed and consumed in increasing quantities.

27.5 The Connection Between Processed Foods and Spiritual Decline

In addition to the physical damage caused by processed foods, there is also a spiritual decline associated with the modern diet. The Bible teaches that we are called to be good stewards of the bodies God has entrusted to us: "Whether therefore ye eat, or drink, or whatsoever ye do, do all to the glory of God." (1 Corinthians 10:31, KJV). When we prioritise convenience over God's natural provision, eating foods that are chemically processed and artificially manufactured, we dishonour the Creator. By choosing foods that are far removed from their original, God-given form, we disconnect ourselves from the divine purpose for our bodies and our health. We are neglecting the principle that our bodies are temples of the Holy Spirit (1 Corinthians 6:19) and are engaging in self-destructive behaviour that diminishes both our physical and spiritual well-being.

27.6 The Road to Restoration: Reclaiming Health Through Whole Foods

To combat the global health crisis caused by processed foods, we must return to a whole-foods-based diet, a diet that honours God's original design for nourishment. This means choosing fresh fruits, vegetables, whole grains, lean meats, and healthy fats, foods that are nourishing, life-giving, and free from artificial additives. In addition to improving physical health, this shift to whole foods can lead to spiritual restoration. When we align our eating habits with God's design, we become more attuned to His will for our lives, strengthening our connection to Him. Eating the foods God created for us not only nourishes our bodies but also helps us honour Him in all that we do, including how we care for our health.

27.7 Conclusion: The Call to Action

The choice to return to whole foods is not just a personal one; it is a global necessity. As we face a world plagued by diet-related diseases, it is time to take action. The global genocide of modern times is not just a crisis of health; it is a crisis of obedience to God's divine design for food and nutrition. It is a call to return to Eden, to embrace God's original plan for nourishment, and to prioritise health in all aspects of our lives. By rejecting the processed food culture and returning to whole, natural foods, we can restore our health and honour God with our bodies. This is not just about avoiding illness; it is about living the abundant life that God intended for us, both physically and spiritually.

Chapter 28

The Role of the Church in Addressing the Global Food Crisis

The rise of processed foods and their devastating impact on global health represents not just a public health crisis, but a spiritual crisis as well. As believers, we are called to be good stewards of the bodies God has entrusted to us, and the Church has an essential role to play in addressing the crisis caused by modern food choices. This chapter explores how the Church can take an active role in leading the charge toward healthier eating habits, educating the congregation, and encouraging a return to God's design for food.

28.1 The Church as a Beacon of Health and Well-being

The Church is a central institution in the life of believers, and it can serve as a powerful vehicle for promoting both physical and spiritual health. Just as the Church preaches the gospel to heal the soul, it can also promote good practices for healing the body. The mission of the Church includes more than just preaching salvation; it also involves the holistic care of individuals, mind, body, and spirit. The Bible teaches that our bodies are temples of the Holy Spirit (1 Corinthians 6:19). It is, therefore, vital that we honour God by treating our bodies with respect and care, including what we eat and how we nourish ourselves.

28.2 Educating the Congregation: A Call to Awareness

One of the most effective ways the Church can address the issue of processed foods and their impact on health is through education. Many believers may not realise the harmful effects of modern eating habits and the global food system. The Church can raise awareness by teaching about the importance of whole, natural foods, the dangers of processed ingredients, and the long-term health consequences of poor dietary choices.

28.2.1 Church Sermons and Bible Studies

Pastors and church leaders can incorporate messages about holistic health into sermons and Bible studies. Drawing from biblical principles, they can explain how the foods we consume impact not only our physical well-being but also our spiritual lives. The Bible offers numerous verses about the importance of healthy living, including verses that address God's design for nourishment and the biblical principles of moderation and self-control. For instance, the story of Daniel and his friends in Babylon (Daniel 1) provides a powerful example of health-conscious living. They chose to eat vegetables and drink water rather than partake in the king's rich, processed foods. This decision honoured God and demonstrated their commitment to spiritual and physical health.

28.2.2 Hosting Health Seminars and Workshops

The Church can also host health seminars and workshops that provide practical guidance on nutrition, meal planning, and cooking healthy foods. These sessions could include guest speakers such as nutritionists, doctors, and health advocates who are passionate about healthy living. Congregants can learn how to make simple but impactful changes to their diets and how these changes can have profound benefits for their overall health.

28.3 Encouraging a Return to Whole, Natural Foods

The return to whole foods is one of the most important actions we can take to combat the global food crisis. The Church has a unique opportunity to encourage believers to embrace a diet based on God's original plan for food, one that is rich in whole grains, fresh vegetables, fruits, and healthy animal products.

28.3.1 Reviving the Practice of Home Gardens

In many parts of the world, especially in developing nations, people once relied on home gardening as a primary source of food. The Church can revive this tradition by encouraging members to plant their own gardens or join community-based agricultural projects. Not only does this reduce the dependence on processed foods, but it also fosters a deeper connection to God's creation. The act of growing one's own food provides a tangible way of participating in God's providence and acknowledging His care for us.

28.3.2 Supporting Local, Sustainable Agriculture

The Church can also advocate for the support of local, sustainable agriculture. By supporting local farmers and food producers who adhere to natural farming methods, congregants can help reduce the demand for industrially processed foods. This can be achieved by purchasing fresh produce from local markets or even by participating in community-supported agriculture (CSA) programs.

28.3.3 Promoting a Whole-Food Diet in Church Events

Another way the Church can lead by example is by offering healthy alternatives during church events. Potlucks, fellowship meals, and church gatherings often feature processed and unhealthy foods. By changing the menu to include more whole foods and healthier options, the Church can model better dietary practices and provide a platform for congregants to experience the benefits of whole-food eating.

28.4 Addressing Social and Economic Barriers

While it is essential to encourage healthier eating, we must also acknowledge that not everyone has access to fresh, whole foods. In many communities, processed foods are cheaper and more readily available than fresh produce. As such, the Church has a role to play in advocating for social justice and supporting efforts to make healthy food accessible to all, particularly those in marginalised communities.

28.4.1 Providing Food Assistance

Many churches already engage in outreach programs that provide food assistance to those in need. By shifting the focus of these programs to include healthy, whole foods, the Church can ensure that the most vulnerable members of society have access to nutritious meals. This could involve collaborating with local food banks, providing fresh produce, or offering healthy meals in food pantries.

28.4.2 Creating Community Gardens and Food Co-ops

Churches can also establish community gardens or food co-ops to address food insecurity. By growing their own produce or pooling resources with other churches, congregations can provide fresh and affordable food to families in need. These initiatives not only help reduce reliance on processed foods but also foster a sense of community and shared responsibility for the well-being of others.

28.5 A Holistic Approach to Health: Body, Mind, and Spirit

The Church's role in promoting health extends beyond food. A holistic approach to health involves caring for the body, mind, and spirit. As we address the global food crisis, it is essential to emphasise the importance of mental health, exercise, sleep, and spiritual growth. Eating healthy is only one part of the equation. God calls us to live balanced lives that honour Him in every area.

28.5.1 Mental Health and Emotional Well-being

The Church can play a significant role in addressing the mental health challenges that arise from the modern diet. Research has shown that nutritional deficiencies and the consumption of highly processed foods can contribute to mood disorders such as depression and anxiety. By teaching about the relationship between diet and mental health, the Church can help individuals make more informed choices that positively impact their emotional and psychological well-being.

28.5.2 Encouraging Exercise and Physical Activity

In addition to promoting healthy eating, the Church can encourage regular physical activity as part of a healthy lifestyle. The Bible teaches us that our bodies are temples of the Holy Spirit, and taking care of them includes staying active and fit. The Church can organise sports activities, walking groups, and fitness programs that help congregants stay active while fostering fellowship and community.

28.6 Conclusion: The Church as a Catalyst for Change

The global food crisis is not just a matter of health; it is a matter of faith. The Church has the unique opportunity to lead the way in encouraging believers to make healthier food choices, return to God's original design for nourishment, and take responsibility for their health. By educating congregants, promoting whole foods, and addressing the social and economic barriers to healthy eating, the Church can help combat the global genocide caused by the processed food industry. As we look to the future, let us embrace the call to honour God with our bodies, to be good stewards of our health, and to lead others toward a healthier, more abundant life. Through education, advocacy, and action, the Church can be a beacon of health and hope in the world.

Chapter 29

Reconnecting with Eden
A Return to God's Original Design for Food

The story of Eden represents not only the beginning of humanity but also the foundation of God's perfect design for our lives, including what we eat. In the Garden of Eden, God provided everything needed for the sustenance and flourishing of Adam and Eve, whole, natural foods that were good for their bodies, minds, and spirits. The fall of man disrupted this harmony, but the original design remains a powerful model for how we should view food today. This chapter explores how reconnecting with the Edenic vision of nourishment can lead to a healthier and more spiritually fulfilling life.

29.1 The Genesis of God's Provision

In the very beginning, God's provision for humanity was simple, pure, and abundant. In Genesis 1:29, God said, *"Behold, I have given you every herb bearing seed, which is upon the face of all the earth, and every tree, in which is the fruit of a tree yielding seed; to you it shall be for meat."* This verse reveals God's initial intention for food: fruits, grains, and seeds were provided as the primary source of nourishment for humanity. There was no need for processed foods or artificial additives. Everything in Eden was created to be in harmony with human health and well-being. The diet was natural, whole, and perfectly designed by the Creator for the optimal health of His creation.

29.2 The Spiritual Significance of Eden's Diet

God's choice of food for Adam and Eve was not arbitrary; it was deeply symbolic. The diet He provided them was clean, pure, and life-sustaining. In their perfect state, there was no need for food preservation, artificial ingredients, or any form of chemical alteration. Their relationship with food mirrored their relationship with God, unblemished, sustaining, and in harmony with creation. In contrast, the processed foods of today often lead to spiritual and physical disconnection from God's original design. Eating artificial, nutrient-depleted foods can result in addiction, poor health, and a weakened spiritual connection. We are often so focused on the "convenience" of modern foods that we lose sight of the way food was intended to nourish and heal us.

29.3 The Fall and the Disruption of God's Design

The fall of humanity, as described in Genesis 3, marked the beginning of the disruption in God's perfect design for human life, including how we approach food. When Adam and Eve sinned, they disobeyed God's command and ate from the forbidden tree. This act of rebellion not only brought spiritual death into the world but also introduced suffering, toil, and corruption into the creation. After the fall, God told Adam that he would now have to "eat bread in the sweat of thy face" (Genesis 3:19). No longer would food be readily abundant and easily gathered. The earth would be cursed, and thorns and thistles would grow, making the cultivation of food more difficult and labour-intensive. This event disrupted the ideal diet designed in Eden, leading to the introduction of processed and artificial foods over time. As humanity moved further from God's original plan, the shift from whole, natural foods to more manipulated and processed foods became inevitable. This disconnection from the Edenic diet has had lasting consequences on human health, both physically and spiritually.

29.4 The Modern Diet: A Far Cry from Eden

Today, the modern diet is characterised by processed and artificial foods that are stripped of their natural nutrients. The average person consumes a large number of refined sugars, trans fats, preservatives, and chemicals, which contribute to a wide range of health issues, including heart disease, diabetes, obesity, and cancer. These processed foods bear little resemblance to the simple, whole foods God intended for us. The food industry has become a massive system driven by profit, cutting corners, and compromising quality. The rise of factory farming, industrial agriculture, and genetically modified organisms (GMOs) has moved us further away from God's original vision for food. What is more alarming is that this shift in diet doesn't just affect our physical health; it impacts our spiritual well-being. Consuming unnatural foods leads to addiction, lack of energy, and mental fog, which can make it harder to connect with God. As we turn to food for comfort or convenience rather than sustenance, we often neglect our spiritual needs and turn inward rather than toward our Creator.

29.5 A Call to Return to Eden: Reclaiming God's Provision

The Bible's message is clear: it is not too late to return to God's original design for food. Just as God's grace provided a way of salvation through Jesus Christ, God's wisdom offers a way to reclaim our health through a return to natural, whole foods.

29.5.1 Rediscovering God's Provision

The first step in returning to Eden is rediscovering the simplicity of God's provision. By choosing foods that are as close to their natural state as possible, fruits, vegetables, whole grains, and lean proteins, we can begin to reclaim the health and vitality that God originally intended for us. This diet does not require complex meal plans or special ingredients, but rather a return to the basics of whole, nutritious foods that nourish our bodies and our spirits.

29.5.2 Biblical Principles of Nourishment

In the Bible, we are encouraged to live in balance and moderation (Philippians 4:5), recognising that our bodies are temples of the Holy Spirit (1 Corinthians 6:19-20). A return to Eden means practicing self-control and discipline when it comes to what we eat. We must resist the temptation of overindulgence and make choices that honour God's design.

29.5.3 Sustainable, Local, and Natural Food Choices

The return to Eden also involves supporting sustainable agriculture and choosing locally grown, organic, and non-GMO foods. By supporting these methods of food production, we honour God's design for a healthy, sustainable world. Choosing natural, whole foods also strengthens our connection to creation and encourages a more holistic approach to life.

29.6 The Spiritual Significance of Reconnecting with Eden

Beyond the physical benefits, reconnecting with Eden through a return to natural foods has profound spiritual implications. As we nourish our bodies with foods designed by God, we honour Him as the Creator and provider of all things. Eating following His original plan helps us to align our actions with His will, promoting a deeper sense of gratitude, contentment, and trust in His provision. Just as the Israelites were commanded to bring their first fruits to God (Exodus 23:19), we can bring our health and well-being back to Him by making choices that reflect our obedience and reverence for His creation.

29.7 Conclusion: Returning to Eden for the Future

The modern food crisis is not only a matter of health; it is a matter of returning to God's original design. As we step away from processed foods and return to whole, natural nourishment, we are reconnecting with the Garden of Eden, a place where God's provision was abundant, pure, and life-giving. God's original vision for food was not only for the sustenance of our bodies but also for the restoration of our spirits. By following His blueprint for eating, we can restore balance to our physical health, reconnect with Him on a deeper level, and contribute to the healing of a broken world. As we return to Eden, we embrace the wisdom of the Creator and walk in the fullness of life He has intended for us.

Chapter 30

Processed Foods and the Human Body
An Unnatural Relationship

The rise of processed foods in modern society has fundamentally altered our relationship with food and, consequently, our health. While God created our bodies to thrive on natural, whole foods, the food industry has transformed what we eat into artificial, chemical-laden products that have no place in God's original design. This chapter explores the biological impact of processed foods, how they affect our bodies, and why this unnatural relationship is leading to a global health crisis.

30.1 The Emergence of Processed Foods

The story of processed foods begins with the Industrial Revolution, during which technological advancements enabled food to be produced on a larger scale. Initially, an innovation designed to preserve food and make it more accessible, it soon evolved into a global industry focused on profit maximisation, often at the expense of health. Processed foods are created by altering raw ingredients through methods such as refining, preserving, artificial flavouring, and packaging. In the process, much of the natural nutrition is stripped away, leaving behind products that are cheap to produce but nutritionally bankrupt. The human body, however, was not designed to consume these artificially created substances. Our systems function optimally when provided with natural, whole foods, those that are nutrient-dense and free from chemicals. The introduction of highly refined sugars, trans fats, additives, and preservatives has created an unnatural relationship between our bodies and the food we eat, leading to a cascade of health problems.

30.2 The Impact of Processed Foods on the Body
30.2.1 Nutrient Depletion and Malnutrition

One of the primary dangers of processed foods is that they are nutrient-poor. While they may appear satisfying, they often contain empty calories, foods that provide little to no nutrition but are loaded with sugar, salt, and unhealthy fats. This nutritional void leaves our bodies lacking essential vitamins and minerals, leading to deficiencies and malnutrition, even in people who consume enough calories. Refined carbohydrates, such as white bread, pasta, and sugar-laden snacks, are quickly digested, causing blood sugar spikes that lead to insulin resistance over time. This promotes the development of chronic diseases like diabetes, heart disease, and obesity. The lack of fibre, vitamins, and minerals in processed foods further weakens the immune system, leaving the body vulnerable to illness and disease.

30.2.2 Inflammation and Chronic Disease

Processed foods contribute to inflammation in the body, which is at the root of many chronic health conditions. Inflammation is a natural response to injury or infection, but when it becomes chronic due to poor diet, it can lead to autoimmune diseases, arthritis, heart disease, and even certain cancers. The excessive consumption of trans fats, found in many processed foods, triggers an inflammatory response in the body. These unhealthy fats disrupt the balance of omega-3 and omega-6 fatty acids in our cells, which play a crucial role in regulating inflammation. When this balance is thrown off, it can lead to systemic inflammation, affecting every organ in the body.

30.3 The Chemical Cocktail: Artificial Additives and Their Effects

The chemical additives used in processed foods are designed to enhance taste, texture, shelf life, and colour. However, many of these chemicals are harmful to human health. The body was not designed to process substances like artificial preservatives, colorants, flavour enhancers, and sweeteners. Over time, the accumulation of these chemicals can overwhelm the body's detoxification systems, leading to liver damage, hormonal imbalances, and even cancer.

30.3.1 Hidden Dangers in Your Food

Common food additives such as monosodium glutamate (MSG), high fructose corn syrup (HFCS), artificial sweeteners, and preservatives like BHA and BHT have been linked to a variety of health issues. Research suggests that MSG, for example, may cause neurological damage and disrupt normal brain function, while HFCS is associated with an increased risk of fatty liver disease, diabetes, and obesity. The harmful effects of these additives are compounded by the lack of nutrients in processed foods, as they further contribute to cellular dysfunction and organ stress. In contrast, whole foods like fruits, vegetables, and whole grains contain antioxidants and phytochemicals that combat free radicals and reduce inflammation, working in harmony with the body's natural healing systems.

30.4 The Psychological Impact of Processed Foods

The effects of processed foods go beyond the physical body. Sugar has a profound impact on our mental health. Studies have shown that the consumption of refined sugars and unhealthy fats can contribute to mood swings, depression, and anxiety. Sugar causes fluctuations in blood sugar levels, which in turn affect the brain's ability to regulate mood. The body becomes addicted to the dopamine hits provided by sugary foods, leading to emotional cravings and dependence on processed foods. Furthermore, the constant consumption of these nutrient-deprived foods can lead to brain fog, fatigue, and difficulty concentrating. The resulting mental fatigue makes it harder for individuals to engage in meaningful spiritual or mental pursuits, creating a cycle of disconnection from both God and oneself.

30.5 Reclaiming the Body: A Return to Natural Foods

The path to healing begins with a return to natural foods, foods that are as close to their original form as possible. This means choosing whole, unprocessed foods that nourish the body and mind, rather than deplete them.

30.5.1 Eating for Healing

We must nourish our bodies with what God has provided: fruits, vegetables, whole grains, and lean proteins. These foods are rich in essential nutrients that support the immune system, improve energy levels, and promote healthy cell regeneration. By prioritising these foods, we can begin to heal the damage caused by processed foods and restore balance to the body.

30.5.2 Detoxification and Restoration

One of the first steps in reversing the damage caused by processed foods is detoxification. This involves eliminating artificial ingredients, sugars, and processed fats from the diet and replacing them with nutrient-dense foods that support the body's natural detox processes. Drinking plenty of water, consuming fibre-rich foods, and incorporating antioxidant-rich fruits like berries, citrus, and leafy greens can help the body remove toxins and restore cellular health.

30.6 Conclusion: Rebuilding a Healthy Relationship with Food

The body was designed to thrive on whole, natural foods that are rich in nutrients and free from harmful chemicals and additives. As we move further away from God's original design for nourishment, we must take action to reclaim our health. By rejecting the processed foods that harm us and embracing the life-giving provisions God has provided, we can restore our bodies, minds, and spirits to their intended state. As we return to Eden's vision for food, we are not only healing ourselves but also reconnecting with the Creator's perfect design. Let us choose life, natural life, and walk in the fullness of health, as God intended.

Chapter 31
The Global Pandemic of Processed Foods
A Crisis of Health and Morality

As the world increasingly consumes processed foods, we are facing a global pandemic not just of health crises, but of moral and spiritual disconnection. While the world continues to push forward in the name of convenience, the long-term consequences are becoming clear: disease, environmental degradation, and a shift in human values. The crisis created by processed foods is not just a matter of nutrition, but of the soul. This chapter explores the far-reaching effects of processed foods on global health and society, and the ethical responsibility of individuals and nations in confronting this moral dilemma.

31.1 A Global Crisis

The global rise of processed foods has brought about a series of interconnected crises, the first being the overwhelming increase in chronic diseases. Over the last century, diseases like diabetes, heart disease, and cancer have skyrocketed, correlating directly with the mass production and consumption of processed foods. What was once considered an indulgence or luxury food has become the staple diet for billions around the world. With their easy accessibility, cheap prices, and pervasive marketing, processed foods are consumed by people from all walks of life, often without realising the impact they are having on their bodies. According to the World Health Organization (WHO), the global obesity rate has more than tripled since 1975. In 2020, it was estimated that 38% of the adult population was overweight, and 13% was obese. This is not just an individual health issue but a societal crisis of massive proportions.

31.1.1 Economic Impact

The economic consequences of a global health crisis rooted in processed food consumption are staggering. As chronic diseases like obesity, diabetes, and heart disease become more prevalent, the economic burden on healthcare systems increases significantly. According to the Centres for Disease Control and Prevention (CDC), the medical costs of obesity alone amount to $147 billion annually in the United States. The food industry's influence on global economies cannot be underestimated. Large corporations that produce processed foods profit immensely, often at the cost of public health. The profits of these industries are derived from making people dependent on food that is designed for profit, not health. This creates a vicious cycle where those who suffer from the long-term effects of processed food are often left to bear the economic costs of their choices.

31.2 The Moral Crisis: Profit Over People

At the core of the processed food industry's success is a fundamental moral failure: the prioritisation of profit over human well-being. The rise of highly processed, nutrient-poor foods is directly tied to the pursuit of profit maximisation in the food industry. Big corporations have exploited consumer ignorance, often marketing products as "healthy" or "natural" despite being laden with sugars, preservatives, and artificial additives. These marketing tactics are designed to create false perceptions about the foods we eat, pushing them as affordable and convenient options while ignoring the long-term health consequences. Ethical concerns also extend to the environmental impact of processed foods. The production of these foods often involves practices that harm the environment, such as monoculture farming, the overuse of chemical pesticides, and deforestation. Moreover, the extensive packaging required for processed foods contributes to massive amounts of waste, polluting the planet and harming ecosystems. The question we must ask ourselves is this: Are we willing to continue supporting an industry that profits off the suffering of people and the planet?

31.3 Processed Foods and the Breakdown of Family and Community

The consequences of the processed food pandemic extend beyond health and economics to affect social structures and community bonds. Food, in its most natural form, is meant to be a source of connection. In biblical times, sharing a meal was a sacred event, a communal experience that brought people together. In contrast, modern society's reliance on processed foods has led to the erosion of these sacred connections.

31.3.1 Disconnection from Nature and God's Design

Processed foods represent a departure from God's original design for food. In Eden, God created whole foods for man to consume, foods that were pure and nourishing for the body. The act of eating in Eden was an act of partaking in God's abundance, not just for physical sustenance but for spiritual communion. In the modern world, however, our disconnect from nature is profound. Many people no longer have a relationship with the land that produces their food. They are consuming products that have been disconnected from their natural origins, fruits, vegetables, grains, and proteins that have been altered so much they bear little resemblance to their original forms. This disconnection has spiritual consequences. When we disconnect from God's creation, we also disconnect from the spiritual nourishment that comes from being in harmony with it. Eating becomes a transaction instead of a sacred experience, and our understanding of food shifts from being a gift to becoming a commodity.

31.3.2 The Family Meal

The breakdown of traditional meals is another consequence of the rise of processed foods. In many households, dinner is no longer a time to gather together and nourish both the body and the soul. Instead, it has become a fast-paced event, with family members eating on the go, often relying on processed, convenience foods. The family meal, once an opportunity for spiritual and emotional connection, is being replaced by individual portions of quick, nutrient-deficient food. This shift not only affects the physical health of families but also disrupts the emotional and spiritual health of individuals within the family unit. Without the sacredness of shared meals, families lose the opportunity for deeper bonding, communication, and spiritual growth.

31.4 Moving Toward a Solution: A Call to Action

The crisis of processed foods cannot be solved overnight, but it requires collective action. As individuals, communities, and nations, we must take responsibility for the food choices we make and the impact they have on our health and the environment.

31.4.1 Reclaiming the Family Table

The first step in confronting the processed food crisis is to reclaim the family table. Families should prioritise shared meals that are rooted in whole, natural foods. In doing so, they not only protect their health but also restore meaning and purpose to the act of eating.

31.4.2 Educating for Change

It is crucial to educate individuals about the dangers of processed foods. From schools to churches, from media to social platforms, the message must be clear: processed foods are not just a personal health risk; they are a moral issue. We must equip people with the knowledge they need to make informed food choices and break free from the cycle of dependence on processed products.

31.4.3 Supporting Ethical Practices

We must also demand more from the food industry. Governments, corporations, and individuals must support practices that prioritise ethical production and sustainability. This means encouraging local farming, organic practices, and fair trade in the food industry. We should also advocate for policies that reduce the environmental impact of food production and eliminate harmful additives and chemicals from processed foods.

31.5 Conclusion: A Moral Responsibility

The global pandemic of processed foods is not just a health crisis; it is a moral crisis. We have a responsibility to not only care for our bodies but also to care for the world around us and the people we share it with. By returning to God's original design for food, by making ethical and healthy choices, we can begin to heal our bodies, our families, our communities, and our planet. The fight against processed foods is a fight for life, for connection, and spiritual well-being. Let us commit to taking that fight seriously, not just for ourselves, but for the generations to come.

Chapter 32

Processed Foods and the Environment
A Destructive Cycle

The widespread consumption of processed foods not only takes a devastating toll on human health but also wreaks havoc on the environment. The global demand for cheap, quick, and convenient food has led to unsustainable agricultural practices, massive deforestation, water depletion, and the pollution of ecosystems. The cycle of destruction fuelled by processed food is a moral and spiritual dilemma that we must confront if we are to restore harmony to the world and return to a more God-centred relationship with creation. This chapter examines the environmental impacts of processed foods, focusing on the interconnectedness of food production, waste, and the broader ecological consequences. It also explores the spiritual implications of exploiting the earth for short-term profit and convenience.

32.1 The Environmental Cost of Processed Foods

The production of processed foods involves several stages, including farming, manufacturing, packaging, and transportation, each of which carries a significant environmental cost. The drive for efficiency and low-cost food production leads to practices that degrade the environment and contribute to climate change.

32.1.1 Industrial Agriculture: A Depletion of Resources

The first stage of producing processed foods begins with the agricultural industry. To meet the demands of an ever-growing global population, industrial farming practices have become the norm. These practices are often unsustainable, relying heavily on the use of pesticides, synthetic fertilisers, and monoculture (growing a single crop over vast areas of land). While these practices yield short-term gains, they exhaust the soil, reduce biodiversity, and require increasing amounts of water and chemical inputs, all of which degrade the environment over time. According to the Food and Agriculture Organization (FAO), monoculture farming is a leading cause of soil erosion, which results in a significant reduction in soil fertility. Over time, this leads to the loss of valuable topsoil, leaving once-productive land barren and unable to produce nutritious crops. Moreover, industrial agriculture relies on vast quantities of water, contributing to the depletion of freshwater sources. In regions where water is already scarce, this exacerbates water scarcity and creates competition for access to this vital resource.

32.1.2 Deforestation for Agriculture

The demand for land to grow food for processed products has led to massive deforestation around the world. Forests, which play a critical role in maintaining biodiversity and regulating the climate, are being cleared to make way for agriculture. According to Global Forest Watch, approximately 10 million hectares of forest are lost each year due to deforestation, much of which is linked to the production of palm oil, soy, and other crops used in processed foods. The clearing of forests not only contributes to carbon emissions but also disrupts entire ecosystems. Many species of plants and animals rely on forests for habitat, and when these ecosystems are destroyed, they are pushed toward extinction. The loss of forests also diminishes the Earth's ability to absorb carbon dioxide, contributing to the intensification of global warming.

32.2 The Global Warming Impact: A Carbon-Intensive Food System

Processed foods are part of a highly carbon-intensive food system. The transportation and packaging of these foods, combined with the energy required for manufacturing, contribute to the accumulation of greenhouse gases in the atmosphere. From farm to table, processed foods have a significant carbon footprint, making them a driving force in global warming.

32.2.1 The Carbon Footprint of Processed Food Production

Every stage of the processed food supply chain generates carbon emissions:

1. **Farming:** Industrial farming practices emit greenhouse gases from the use of fertilisers, pesticides, and the operation of large machinery.
2. **Manufacturing:** The processing of raw materials into packaged foods often requires significant energy inputs. High-temperature cooking, drying, and packaging processes contribute to carbon emissions.
3. **Transportation:** Processed foods are typically transported long distances across the globe. Whether by truck, ship, or airplane, the transportation of these goods uses fossil fuels, further adding to the carbon footprint.
4. **Packaging:** The use of non-biodegradable plastic packaging for processed foods exacerbates the environmental crisis. Plastics are difficult to recycle and often end up in landfills or oceans, polluting the planet.

32.2.2 Food Waste and Its Impact

A significant percentage of processed foods never even reach the dinner plate, contributing to a substantial global waste problem. According to the United Nations Environment Programme (UNEP), one-third of all food produced is wasted. This waste represents not only the loss of food but also the resources (water, land, energy) used in its production. The environmental toll of food waste is profound. Landfills are the largest source of methane emissions, a potent greenhouse gas. When food rots in landfills, it produces methane as it decomposes anaerobically. Methane is over 80 times more potent than carbon dioxide over 20 years.

32.3 A Spiritual Reflection: Our Relationship with Creation

The environmental destruction wrought by the processed food industry reflects a broken relationship between humanity and the earth. In Genesis 1:28, God commands humanity to "be fruitful and multiply, and fill the earth and subdue it". This call to steward the earth was never meant to be an exploitative or destructive relationship but one of care, respect, and nurturing. When we engage in practices that harm the earth, whether through the destruction of forests, the pollution of waters, or the depletion of natural resources, we are violating the very command God gave to humanity. The exploitation of the earth to produce processed foods is an affront to God's design for creation. It is a denial of the responsibility to be good stewards of the planet and its resources. In Romans 8:19-22, Paul speaks of creation itself groaning in anticipation of redemption. The earth longs for restoration, and as Christians, we are called to be agents of that restoration. The food we consume and the way we treat creation are integral to this process. If we are to heal the planet, we must first recognise our role in creation care and turn away from practices that harm it.

32.4 Solutions: A Call for Sustainable Food Practices

To combat the environmental destruction caused by processed foods, we must embrace more sustainable, ethical food systems. Several key strategies can help mitigate the negative environmental impact of our diets:

32.4.1 Supporting Local and Organic Agriculture

One of the most effective ways to reduce the environmental footprint of our food is to support local and organic agriculture. Organic farming practices rely on fewer chemicals and promote soil health, biodiversity, and water conservation. By purchasing locally produced food, we can reduce the carbon emissions associated with transportation and support farmers who prioritise sustainable practices.

32.4.2 Reducing Food Waste

In addition to changing what we eat, we must also address the waste associated with food. Governments, corporations, and individuals must work together to reduce food waste at every stage of the food system. This includes better food storage, improved packaging, and efforts to donate excess food to those in need.

32.4.3 Promoting Plant-Based Diets

Another key solution is to embrace more plant-based diets, which generally have a lower environmental impact than animal-based foods. Shifting toward plant-based eating can reduce greenhouse gas emissions, conserve water, and protect ecosystems.

32.4.4 Sustainable Packaging

The packaging used for processed foods is a significant contributor to environmental pollution. The use of plastic, particularly single-use plastic, must be reduced. Companies should be encouraged to adopt sustainable packaging solutions, such as biodegradable materials or recyclable options.

32.5 Conclusion: A Call for Ethical Consumption

The environmental consequences of processed foods are undeniable. However, as consumers, we have the power to influence the food system by choosing sustainable and ethical options. By supporting organic and local agriculture, reducing food waste, and embracing plant-based diets, we can contribute to the healing of the planet and restore our relationship with the earth. In the process, we fulfil our moral and spiritual duty to be faithful stewards of the world God has entrusted to us. Let us commit to consuming with a purpose, to honour God's creation and to nourish both our bodies and the planet.

Chapter 33

The Biblical Call to Care for Our Bodies
A Temple of the Holy Spirit

In the broader context of humanity's relationship with food, it is essential to recognise that the physical body itself is a vessel, a temple entrusted to us by God. Just as we are called to care for the earth and all its creatures, we are also instructed to treat our bodies with honour and respect. The biblical perspective on the body underscores its sacredness and calls for its proper care, a task made more urgent in an age where processed foods threaten to undermine our health and well-being. This chapter explores the spiritual and biblical foundation for caring for our bodies and emphasises how the consumption of harmful, processed foods is contrary to God's design for our physical health. We will delve into key scriptures that instruct us on the importance of treating our bodies as temples of the Holy Spirit, and how the choices we make about food impact not only our physical health but also our spiritual vitality.

33.1 The Body as a Temple: A Sacred Responsibility

In 1 Corinthians 6:19-20, the Apostle Paul writes: *"Do you not know that your bodies are temples of the Holy Spirit, who is in you, whom you have received from God? You are not your own; you were bought at a price. Therefore, honour God with your bodies."* This powerful scripture emphasises the sacred nature of the body. Our bodies are not merely physical structures but are inhabited by the Holy Spirit, making them sacred vessels entrusted to us by God. The responsibility to care for our bodies is not simply a matter of aesthetics or self-interest; it is a spiritual duty. Just as we are called to honour God in all aspects of our lives, we must also honour Him by taking care of the physical bodies He has given us. The choices we make in what we eat, how we treat our bodies, and how we nourish ourselves should reflect our faithfulness to God's calling. In this way, the physical body is a sacred space, and its well-being is directly connected to our spiritual health. By caring for our bodies, we are honouring God's design for us, which includes the wise stewardship of our health and well-being. However, modern habits, particularly the consumption of processed foods, can undermine this sacred responsibility and degrade the quality of life God intends for us.

33.2 The Dangers of Processed Foods: A Hindrance to Physical and Spiritual Health

In the modern world, the processed food industry has led to an overwhelming shift in what we eat. These foods are typically high in refined sugars, unhealthy fats, and artificial additives, substances that can wreak havoc on the body. The regular consumption of such foods contributes to a myriad of health issues, including obesity, heart disease, diabetes, and other chronic conditions. Beyond the obvious physical risks, the consumption of processed foods also has a spiritual dimension. When we indulge in foods that are harmful to our bodies, we are, in essence, dishonouring the temple God has entrusted to us. Ephesians 5:29-30 states: *"After all, no one ever hated their own body, but they feed and care for their body, just as Christ does the church—for we are members of his body."* The verse highlights the principle of nurturing the body as we would cherish and care for a loved one. When we make poor dietary choices, we ignore this calling and fail to treat our bodies with the respect they deserve. Processed foods, by their nature, are often void of nutritional value and are created for profit, rather than for the genuine well-being of the consumer. These foods are not designed to nourish but to satisfy fleeting cravings, and their overconsumption has led to widespread malnutrition, despite the abundance of food. Furthermore, these foods are addictive by design, often using refined sugars and additives that trigger the brain's reward centres, encouraging overeating and a cycle of dependence. This is not simply a physical struggle; it is also a spiritual battle. 1 Corinthians 6:12 says, *"I have the right to do anything,"* you say—*but not everything is beneficial. I have the right to do anything—but I will not be mastered by anything."* The overconsumption of processed foods can easily become a form of idolatry, where the pursuit of temporary pleasure overrides our commitment to honouring God with our bodies.

33.3 Caring for the Body: A Biblical Perspective on Nutrition and Health

The Bible provides us with foundational wisdom for caring for our bodies, emphasising the importance of nutrition, balance, and moderation. From the dietary laws in the Old Testament to the principles of healthy living found in the New Testament, scripture teaches us that we are to prioritise the well-being of our physical bodies.

33.3.1 The Diet of Eden: God's Original Design

In the Garden of Eden, God gave Adam and Eve a perfect diet of fruits, vegetables, and plants. Genesis 1:29 says: *"Then God said, 'I give you every seed-bearing plant on the face of the whole earth and every tree that has fruit with seed in it. They will be yours for food.'"* This was God's original design for human nutrition: fresh, plant-based, whole foods that nourish the body and align with His purpose for creation. In contrast to the processed foods that have come to dominate the modern diet, Eden's diet was designed to sustain health, promote longevity, and provide spiritual nourishment. The abundance of natural, unprocessed foods reflects the wholeness of God's creation and His desire for His people to live in harmony with the earth. While the dietary laws given to Israel in the Old Testament (e.g., in Leviticus 11) were specific to the Jewish people, they offer valuable principles that align with a healthy, God-centred diet. Foods that are clean, unadulterated, and wholesome are preferred in scripture, promoting both physical and spiritual vitality.

33.3.2 Moderation and Balance in Food Consumption

Scripture also teaches the importance of moderation in all things, including food. Proverbs 25:27 says: *"It is not good to eat too much honey, nor is it honourable to search out matters that are too deep."* This principle of moderation encourages a balanced approach to food consumption. Overindulgence, especially in the form of processed foods, disrupts the body's natural balance and leads to health problems. In 1 Corinthians 10:31, Paul reminds us that, *"Whether you eat or drink or whatever you do, do it all for the glory of God."* This means that even in our food choices, we are called to glorify God by making choices that support our health and well-being. Our bodies are meant to serve as vessels for His purposes, and we honour God when we take care of our physical health through nutritious eating.

33.4 The Spiritual Power of Healthy Living

When we commit to treating our bodies as temples and embrace a nutritious, balanced diet, we align ourselves more closely with God's purpose for our lives. Healthy living not only enhances our physical health but also empowers us to fulfil God's calling on our lives more effectively. Our bodies are instruments of service, and when we nourish them, we are better equipped to serve God and others. In Romans 12:1, Paul urges us to *"offer your bodies as a living sacrifice, holy and pleasing to God—this is your true and proper worship."* Worshipping God with our bodies means taking care of them and honouring God's original design for health and well-being. It means stepping away from the destructive cycle of processed foods and choosing to embrace the life-giving nourishment found in God's creation.

33.5 Conclusion: Honouring God with Our Bodies

As Christians, our journey toward health and well-being is not just about physical appearance or even longevity; it is about honouring God with our bodies, treating them as temples of the Holy Spirit. The consumption of processed foods and the neglect of our bodies is a spiritual issue, and by choosing to live healthily, we embrace the responsibility God has given us to care for His creation. Let us return to the biblical vision of health, where our bodies are nourished by whole, natural foods that align with God's perfect design. By doing so, we not only promote our physical well-being but also reflect the glory of God in every aspect of our lives, including the food we eat.

Chapter 34

The Impact of Processed Foods on Mental Health
A Silent Crisis

As the world continues to grapple with rising health challenges, one aspect of the human experience that has been largely overlooked in the conversation about processed foods is mental health. While we are acutely aware of the physical dangers of processed foods, obesity, heart disease, and diabetes, there is a silent crisis unfolding in the realm of mental well-being. In recent years, research has revealed a growing connection between the consumption of processed foods and the rise in mental health disorders. This chapter explores how processed foods are affecting not only our bodies but also our minds, and how this crisis ties back to God's original intention for our diets.

34.1 The Modern Epidemic: Processed Foods and Rising Mental Health Issues

Mental health issues such as depression, anxiety, ADHD, and even schizophrenia are on the rise worldwide, and many experts are beginning to suspect that poor diet is a significant contributing factor. Studies have shown that diets high in processed foods and low in nutritional value can significantly affect brain chemistry, leading to mood swings, irritability, and cognitive decline. The nutrients in the food we consume play a critical role in brain function, and when we consistently deprive ourselves of essential vitamins, minerals, and fatty acids, our mental health suffers. Refined sugars, trans fats, and artificial additives are found in abundance in processed foods, and these substances have been linked to inflammation in the brain. Inflammation is known to play a central role in many mental health conditions, including depression. Furthermore, the overconsumption of sugar has been shown to harm neurotransmitter function, the chemicals in our brain that regulate mood, memory, and cognition. The modern Western diet, rich in processed foods, has become a significant risk factor for mental health disorders, and it is no coincidence that countries with higher consumption of processed foods also have higher rates of mental health issues. This crisis is not only personal but also societal, affecting families, communities, and entire nations.

34.2 The Link Between Processed Foods and Depression

One of the most alarming connections researchers have uncovered is the relationship between processed foods and depression. People who consume a diet high in processed foods are more likely to experience symptoms of depression than those who eat a more whole-food-based diet. Several studies have shown that the consumption of processed foods leads to changes in the gut microbiome, the ecosystem of bacteria living in the digestive system. This disruption in gut health can influence the gut-brain axis, the communication pathway between the gut and the brain, and has been linked to an increased risk of depressive symptoms. Some studies suggest that a dietary pattern rich in processed foods can increase the likelihood of chronic inflammation, which is a key player in the development of depression. As inflammation increases, the brain becomes more susceptible to mood disorders, and the symptoms of depression worsen. The Bible speaks of joy and peace of mind as fruits of the Spirit. *"The fruit of the Spirit is love, joy, peace..."* (Galatians 5:22). While there are spiritual aspects to these qualities, the food we consume can play a direct role in our mental and emotional state. When we eat foods that promote inflammation and hinder proper brain function, we make ourselves more vulnerable to emotional distress and mental health struggles.

34.3 Anxiety and Processed Foods: A Hidden Contributor

Anxiety is another mental health issue that has been linked to the consumption of processed foods. Just as depression has been connected to a poor diet, anxiety, a condition that affects millions worldwide, is exacerbated by unhealthy eating habits. Studies have shown that refined carbohydrates, sugary foods, and artificial additives can trigger or worsen symptoms of anxiety.

Processed foods, particularly those that are high in sugar, lead to blood sugar spikes and crashes, which can affect mood stability and lead to irritability, stress, and heightened anxiety levels. Low blood sugar, which often follows the initial sugar rush, can cause feelings of nervousness and unease. This pattern of blood sugar instability can contribute to a constant cycle of heightened anxiety. Furthermore, the gut-brain connection again plays a pivotal role in anxiety. When the gut microbiome is unbalanced due to poor diet, it can lead to symptoms of anxiety as well as other cognitive disturbances. Proverbs 12:25 says, *"Anxiety in the heart of man causes depression, but a good word makes it glad."* This scripture highlights the link between our emotional state and our mental health, acknowledging the powerful effects anxiety can have on our overall well-being. The process of healing from anxiety, then, may not only involve spiritual renewal and emotional support but also nutritional healing. A balanced diet of whole, nutrient-dense foods can provide the body with the tools it needs to maintain stable blood sugar levels, reduce inflammation, and support the health of the brain and gut.

34.4 The Role of Omega-3 Fatty Acids and Nutrient-Dense Foods in Mental Health

One of the most promising nutritional approaches to addressing mental health issues is the incorporation of omega-3 fatty acids into the diet. These essential fats, found in foods like fatty fish, flaxseeds, and chia seeds, have been shown to have a profound impact on brain function and mood regulation. Omega-3s are key building blocks of the brain, and they help reduce inflammation in the brain, which is linked to mood disorders like depression and anxiety. Furthermore, a diet rich in fruits, vegetables, whole grains, and lean proteins provides the necessary vitamins and minerals to support brain health. Nutrients such as B vitamins, magnesium, and zinc are essential for the production and function of neurotransmitters that regulate mood and mental health. A diet lacking these essential nutrients, often found in processed foods, can lead to cognitive decline, poor memory, and mental fatigue. This underscores the importance of returning to the biblical model of eating, where natural, whole foods form the foundation of our nutrition. Genesis 1:29, God's original command to humanity, provides us with a timeless blueprint: a plant-based diet rich in fruits and vegetables, which promotes both physical and mental health.

34.5 Restoring Balance: Healing the Mind and Body Through Proper Nutrition

The restoration of mental health, like the restoration of physical health, requires holistic care. Just as we seek to honour God with our bodies by avoiding processed foods, we must also consider the role that nutrition plays in maintaining mental peace. A whole-food, nutrient-rich diet can help reduce symptoms of anxiety, depression, and cognitive decline. By shifting away from processed, inflammatory foods and toward a more natural, plant-based diet, we can restore balance in both the body and the mind.

34.6 Conclusion: A Biblical Path to Healing and Wholeness

The crisis of mental health in modern society is multifaceted, but one of the key contributors is our modern diet, particularly the overconsumption of processed foods. Scripture teaches us that we are to care for our bodies as temples of the Holy Spirit, and that includes our mental and emotional health. As we begin to recognise the importance of proper nutrition in sustaining not just physical health but mental health as well, we can begin the journey toward healing and wholeness, spiritually, emotionally, and physically. Let us return to God's original plan for food, choosing nourishment that honours Him and supports the well-being of our bodies and minds. By doing so, we can experience true peace and joy, both of which are the fruits of living in alignment with God's will.

Chapter 35
The Myth of Fortified Foods
A Trojan Horse in Your Diet

In a world that increasingly relies on science to mend what industry has broken, "fortified" foods have become a household term. Cereal boxes scream promises of added iron, milk cartons boast of vitamin D, and bread comes enriched with folic acid. To the average consumer, this appears to be a noble effort, correcting deficiencies and bolstering nutrition. But behind the marketing veneer lies a deeper problem: fortification often masks the real issue, that our food has been so processed and stripped of natural nutrients that it needs to be artificially repaired.

The Deception of Fortification

Fortification is not the same as natural nourishment. When nutrients are artificially added back into food, they are often synthetic versions of what once existed naturally. The body may not absorb or utilise these forms effectively. Moreover, they frequently exist in isolation, without the accompanying cofactors (such as enzymes, fibre, or trace minerals) that natural whole foods provide. In this way, fortified foods are like bandaging a wound caused by a sword we refuse to remove. We are led to believe that deficiencies can be addressed by sprinkling isolated vitamins onto lifeless food. But God's original design in Eden didn't rely on chemistry labs; it relied on whole, living, plant-based nutrition. Genesis 1:29 says, *"Behold, I have given you every herb bearing seed, which is upon the face of all the earth... to you it shall be for meat."* Nothing needed to be fortified; it was already *full*.

Fortification and Corporate Control

The food industry's use of fortification is not simply a health initiative; it's also a control mechanism. By creating processed foods that must be "enhanced," corporations retain ownership over the formula, the process, and the dependency of the public. You cannot fortify an apple, but you can manipulate breakfast cereal until it becomes a proprietary blend. In doing so, industry shifts the power from farms to factories. This dynamic also affects global aid. Fortified foods are exported to "solve" malnutrition in developing nations, while local, natural farming is discouraged. Entire populations are made reliant on powdered milk or fortified rice, stripping them of sovereignty over their food systems.

Side Effects and Overdose

Fortification can also be harmful. Excess iron, for example, is linked to heart disease, while high doses of synthetic folic acid may mask signs of vitamin B12 deficiency, leading to nerve damage. Children, especially, are vulnerable to the cumulative effects of eating multiple fortified products daily. When God designed the human body, He also designed the food to fit it, not in artificial abundance, but in balanced wholeness. Proverbs 25:16 offers a caution: *"Hast thou found honey? Eat so much as is sufficient for thee."* More is not always better, especially when it's man-made.

The Biblical Model of Natural Provision

God's Word is filled with agricultural imagery and food metaphors, not centred on human alteration, but on divine provision. The Promised Land is described as flowing with milk and honey, not pills and powder. Jesus fed the multitudes with five loaves and two fish, not a "nutrient-fortified product." In every biblical instance, nourishment was real, whole, and sufficient. The deception of fortified foods is not that they contain nutrients, but that they distract from what has been lost, and more dangerously, they pretend to be better than what God originally made.

Reclaiming Wholeness

To reverse the genocide of our health, we must return to wholeness, whole foods, whole understanding, and whole trust in God's design. This means avoiding so-called "nutritional band-aids" and instead pursuing what was never broken. The solution to a man-made problem is rarely another man-made invention. If the body is the temple of the Holy Spirit (1 Corinthians 6:19), then what we feed it should reflect the reverence due to the One who designed it. Fortification is not a fix; it is often a façade.

Chapter 36

How the Microwave Changed Everything
From Fire to Frequency

At first glance, the microwave oven appears to be one of the greatest inventions of the 20th century. With the push of a button, meals that once took hours are ready in minutes. It fits the rhythm of a fast-paced world, efficient, compact, and easy. But hidden beneath the hum of convenience is a far more complex and concerning story: one that reveals how the method of cooking can alter not only the food but the very health of those who consume it.

The Birth of a Machine, The Death of a Flame

Traditional cooking, fire, boiling, roasting, has been with humanity since the days of Eden. It preserves the sanctity of food's molecular structure while enhancing its natural nutrients. Fire was God's gift to man (see Genesis 8:20–21), a tool to prepare food while retaining its God-given integrity. Microwaves, by contrast, work on an entirely different principle. They use electromagnetic radiation in the microwave frequency range to cause water molecules in food to vibrate rapidly, generating heat from the inside out. While this may sound clever, the real question is: *what does this process do to the food itself, and us?*

Molecular Mayhem

Studies have shown that microwave radiation can alter the molecular structure of food. Proteins can be denatured in abnormal ways, vitamins can be destroyed, and fats can be transformed into harmful compounds. A 1992 study in *The Journal of Food Chemistry* found significant decreases in antioxidants in vegetables microwaved versus those steamed or boiled. Another study published in *The Lancet* in the 1980s noted structural degradation in microwaved human milk, which affected immunity-boosting properties vital for infants. The problem is not just *what* is being cooked, but *how*. God created food to be consumed as part of a living ecosystem. When its design is tampered with at a molecular level, the consequences go beyond the visible.

Speed at a Cost

Microwaving appeals to the spirit of the age, instant results, minimal effort, and no relationship with the process. But this is not how God operates. The kingdom of God is compared to *sowing*, *waiting*, and *harvesting*, slow, intentional, and relational (Galatians 6:7-9). Microwaves represent the opposite, a shortcut that bypasses wisdom. The loss of traditional cooking has contributed to the breakdown of family meals, community, and connection. Where once meals were prepared with care, love, and time, we now heat processed products alone, standing by the microwave, phones in hand. A slow-cooked stew requires thought. A microwaved dinner requires only a timer.

Health Implications of Microwave Cooking

Some of the potential health concerns associated with long-term microwave usage include:

- Nutrient depletion: Water-soluble vitamins like B12, C, and others are particularly vulnerable
- Chemical leaching: When microwaving food in plastic containers, harmful substances like BPA can seep into the food
- Increased oxidative stress: Irregular heating and breakdown of food molecules can introduce oxidative compounds that increase aging and inflammation

All these factors work silently against the body, contributing to the slow, methodical destruction of health: a hidden genocide in the kitchen.

Biblical Cooking — A Sacred Act

Cooking, in Scripture, is often a sacred activity. Abraham prepared a meal for the Lord (Genesis 18:6–8), and Jesus cooked fish over a fire for His disciples after the resurrection (John 21:9). These were not rushed moments; they were personal, intimate, and infused with relationship. The act of preparing food God's way invites us to slow down, to connect, to be intentional. Microwaves, on the other hand, reflect the world's gospel of speed and detachment. They might save time, but often at the cost of both health and holiness.

Reclaiming the Flame

It's time to reclaim the flame, not only literally, but spiritually. Whether it's a wood stove, a slow cooker, or a humble pot on a gas burner, the method of preparation matters. It is not merely about taste or nostalgia; it's about integrity, preserving what God created rather than distorting it. The war on human health is not always fought with weapons; it is often waged with appliances. Let us return to a slower, better way of feeding ourselves and our families. Just as Elijah called fire from heaven (1 Kings 18), perhaps the modern Church must once again call for the fire of God, not only to consume sacrifices, but to sanctify kitchens.

Chapter 37

Baby Formula and the Breakdown of Generational Health

For centuries, the miracle of breastfeeding has been central to human survival and infant development. It was designed by God as the perfect food, custom-made by each mother, in real time, to nourish and protect her child. Yet in the last hundred years, a global shift has occurred. Baby formula, once a tool of last resort, has become a billion-dollar industry and the new norm in many parts of the world. But this shift is not without consequences. It has contributed to a multi-generational erosion of immunity, health, and divine design.

The Rise of the Substitute

The 20th century saw the rise of industrial food science, and with it, the commercialisation of infant formula. Originally developed for orphanages or situations where mothers couldn't breastfeed, formula quickly became widespread, thanks in large part to aggressive marketing campaigns. Companies positioned formula as "scientific," "modern," and even "superior" to breast milk. Hospitals were incentivised to distribute free samples, and medical professionals were recruited as spokespersons. The consequences? Breastfeeding rates plummeted. Generations of infants were raised on processed powders instead of living nourishment. And the world changed, quietly but profoundly.

What's Really in the Can?

Baby formula is typically made from highly processed cow's milk, soy protein isolates, vegetable oils, synthetic vitamins, and added sugars. While it may sustain life, it does not replicate the complexity of breast milk, which contains living enzymes, hormones, antibodies, stem cells, and microbiota unique to each child's needs. Formula-fed infants often experience:

- Increased risk of infections and allergies
- Higher rates of obesity and diabetes later in life
- Reduced bonding with the mother
- Altered gut microbiome development
- Lower IQ scores, in some long-term studies

And yet, society continues to normalise it, package it, and push it, even in impoverished regions where access to clean water is limited, making formula not only inferior but dangerous.

A Spiritual Attack on the Seed

From a biblical standpoint, this is not just a health issue; it is a spiritual attack on the seed of the next generation. In Exodus

2, we see how Moses' mother nursed him even while under threat from Pharaoh's decree. She understood that what she fed him would shape who he became. In contrast, today's Pharaoh is subtle. He does not kill the seed with swords, but with substitutes. God designed mothers to be the first nourisher, teacher, and protector of life. Breastfeeding is not just biology; it is discipleship. Formula, in many ways, replaces this God-ordained intimacy with industrial detachment.

The Economics of Dependency

The formula industry thrives on creating dependency. Once a mother's milk dries up, or never comes in due to stress, misinformation, or early hospital separation, she is locked into buying a product for months or years. This is especially cruel in developing nations, where formula companies have targeted vulnerable populations, encouraging them to abandon traditional breastfeeding practices for a product they can barely afford. Meanwhile, global aid organisations, instead of empowering natural breastfeeding, often distribute formula donations, creating entire generations dependent on Western food systems, instead of God's original design.

Restoring God's Model

This chapter is not meant to shame mothers who have used formula out of necessity. Grace and wisdom are always needed. But it is a call to see the bigger picture: a war is being waged on the cradle. What should be sacred has been commodified. Breast milk is a covenantal gift from God, a living supply of exactly what a baby needs at every stage of growth. No lab can replicate it. No company can manufacture it. It is divine. Isaiah 66:11 beautifully captures this image: *"That ye may suck, and be satisfied with the breasts of her consolations; that ye may milk out, and be delighted with the abundance of her glory."* To stop the genocide of human health, we must return to generational wisdom. Let grandmothers, midwives, and wise women teach again. Let churches support mothers. Let fathers honour the role of the nurturer. Let governments protect instead of promote industry. The restoration of a generation begins not in school, but at the breast. There, the body is built, the brain is shaped, and the spirit is stabilised. There, the war is either won or lost.

Chapter 38
From Earth to Asphalt
The Death of the Family Garden

Once upon a time, nearly every home had a small garden. Whether urban or rural, the backyard bore life, tomatoes climbing wooden stakes, herbs sunning themselves in clay pots, children pulling carrots from the soil with dirt under their nails. It was more than food, it was formation. It taught patience, provision, and participation in the cycle of life. But somewhere along the way, the garden was replaced with concrete patios, synthetic lawns, parking bays, and supermarket dependency. This chapter is a lament and a call to action. For in the slow disappearance of the family garden, a vital thread of human dignity and divine connection has been severed.

The Garden Was God's First Classroom

Before there was a tabernacle, there was a garden. Eden was both a sanctuary and a school. God placed man not in a palace or a factory, but in a garden to "work it and take care of it" (Genesis 2:15). In doing so, He established agriculture as the first profession and stewardship of the earth as a sacred responsibility. In the garden, Adam learned not only how to tend plants but how to hear God. There is something about planting, watering, and waiting that forms a soul. Gardening trains the heart in patience, discipline, and gratitude, qualities rapidly vanishing in our microwave, mobile-app-driven world.

Industrialisation and the Loss of Soil

As cities expanded and economies industrialised, families migrated from plots to apartments, from gardens to grocery stores. The soil beneath their feet turned to tar, and with it, their awareness of seasons, nutrition, and sustainability faded. Supermarkets became the new harvest field, stocked with produce flown in from thousands of kilometres away, often sprayed, waxed, and genetically altered. Children now believe carrots come in plastic bags and strawberries are available year-round. The convenience is seductive, but the cost is catastrophic.

What the Garden taught that the store forgot

1. **Seasonal Wisdom Gardens** teach when things grow and why they sometimes don't. Supermarkets teach that you can have anything, anytime, if you have money.
2. **Work-Eat Connection.** The garden connects effort to reward. You harvest what you sow, an echo of Galatians 6:7. In the store, the link between labour and provision is severed, numbing both gratitude and humility.

3. **Community and Care Neighbourhood** gardens, used to foster sharing and storytelling. Now, fences and fast food isolate us even from those next doors.
4. **Biodiversity and Immunity Growing** your own food introduces your body to local microbes and living soil, key to a healthy immune system. Sterile, chemical-laden produce does not.

The Asphalt Genocide

The paving over of gardens is not just environmental; it is spiritual. It is the erasure of God's first teaching space. It is no accident that food deserts exist in the poorest areas, where concrete dominates and fresh produce is scarce. It is no coincidence that lifestyle diseases like diabetes, obesity, and heart conditions spike where no one knows how to grow their food. This is a silent genocide, a cultural loss masked as progress.

Return to Eden — One Pot at a Time

Reviving the garden doesn't require hectares. A single tomato plant on a balcony is a declaration of war against global food control. A pot of basil on the windowsill is a whisper of Eden. Communities can reclaim rooftops, churches can host garden days, and schools can turn empty spaces into learning farms. The solution to world hunger is not only in large-scale aid, but in small-scale faithfulness. If every family grew just 10% of their food, global health and economics would shift dramatically.

A Prophetic Picture

In Amos 9:14, God promises: *"They will plant vineyards and drink their wine; they will make gardens and eat their fruit."* This is not just agricultural, it's redemptive. Reclaiming the garden is reclaiming God's rhythm. It is a prophetic act that says, "We will not bow to convenience. We will plant again." Let the Church lead. Let elders teach the young how to sow and reap. Let homes echo once more with laughter and labour among the rows of green. The family garden is not just about vegetables. It is about vision. It is about returning to the roots, before the poison, before the profit, before the plastic. It is about defying the genocide, one seed at a time.

Chapter 39

Pharmaceuticals in the Food Chain
A Silent War on the Body

It is one thing for medicine to heal the sick; it is quite another when pharmaceuticals silently lace the daily bread of a generation. In this chapter, we uncover a disturbing and underreported truth: pharmaceuticals are no longer confined to hospitals and pharmacies. They have infiltrated the food chain. From livestock injected with hormones to crops sprayed with chemical cocktails, humanity now consumes traces of drugs without a prescription, day after day, bite after bite. This is not healing. This is harm disguised as health.

Hormones in Livestock: Growth at What Cost?

In the race for profit, the agriculture industry has turned to pharmaceutical shortcuts. Livestock are no longer simply fed; they are medicated.

- Growth Hormones are given to cattle to accelerate weight gain.

- Oestrogen and testosterone derivatives are used to speed up puberty in animals, leading to faster turnover.
- Antibiotics are administered routinely, not to treat illness, but to prevent it in overcrowded and unsanitary conditions.

These drugs do not disappear once the animal is slaughtered. Residues remain in the meat, milk, and eggs, passing on chemical traces to the consumer.

Long-term exposure to these residues has been linked to:

- Early puberty in children
- Hormonal imbalances in adults
- Antibiotic resistance in global populations
- Endocrine system disruption
- Infertility and reproductive disorders

And yet, regulatory systems in many countries allow it. Why? Because food is no longer about nourishment, it's about output.

Antibiotic Resistance: A Global Time Bomb

One of the gravest consequences of pharmaceuticals in food is the rise of antibiotic resistance. When antibiotics are used routinely in animal feed, bacteria adapt and evolve. These superbugs then enter the human population, rendering our medicines powerless. The World Health Organization has warned that antibiotic resistance may become the next global pandemic, potentially killing more people annually than cancer by 2050. And it started, not in hospitals, but in feedlots.

Chemical Farming and Pesticide Residues

Beyond meat, even the fruits and vegetables we eat are now chemical-laden. Pesticides, herbicides, and fungicides often contain pharmaceutical-grade ingredients that alter not only pests but also human biology. Glyphosate, the world's most used herbicide, has been linked to:

- Cancer
- Gut microbiome disruption
- Neurodevelopmental disorders
- Kidney and liver damage

Yet it continues to be used on staple crops like wheat, corn, and soy, making it nearly impossible to avoid without careful sourcing.

Biblical Warning: The Poison in the Pot

In 2 Kings 4:40, the sons of the prophets cry out to Elisha, *"O man of God, there is death in the pot!"* This verse echoes today's reality. The food pot has become tainted, corrupted by unseen agents that claim to improve, but in truth, degrade. The pharmaceutical invasion of the food chain is a modern example of this spiritual principle. What should nourish now slowly poisons. What should give life now contributes to disease.

Why is no one talking about it?

The silence is strategic. The same corporations that profit from pharmaceutical agriculture also invest heavily in media, medicine, and government policy. They control the narrative. Speak up, and you risk being labelled a conspiracy theorist. Stay silent, and the masses continue to consume, sickening themselves slowly, dependently, and profitably. It is a genius model of control: poison them through food, then sell them the cure through drugs.

The Way of Escape

God never intended for man to live on synthetics. In Genesis, He gave Adam and Eve every seed-bearing plant for food (Genesis 1:29). No injections. No pills. Just pure, living matter designed to sustain and heal. To escape this pharmaceutical food trap:

1. Buy organic or local where possible.
2. Avoid processed meat products and fast foods.
3. Support regenerative and ethical farming.
4. Educate your family on food labels and hidden chemicals.
5. Detox regularly with natural herbs and fasting.

A Holy Diet in a Corrupt World

Daniel and his friends in Babylon chose vegetables and water over the king's defiled meat and wine (Daniel 1:8–16). After ten days, they looked healthier and wiser than all the others. That was no accident. It was divine nutrition. Today, the spirit of Babylon lives on, offering contaminated delicacies and calling them good. But like Daniel, we can choose differently. We can refuse the king's portion. We can reclaim purity in what we eat. The war is not just on our minds or spirits; it is on our stomachs. But if we eat with discernment, we eat with dominion. Let every meal be a protest. Let every choice be a stand. Let your plate be holy ground.

Chapter 40

Digital Disconnection
The Forgotten Hunger of the Soul

While the world obsesses over the physical dangers of food, an even deeper famine is spreading silently across humanity, a famine of connection, stillness, and spiritual nourishment. In the age of ultra-connectivity, people are lonelier than ever. Screens dominate dinner tables. Notifications interrupt prayer. Families sit together, but hearts are far apart. We have never had so much information and yet so little wisdom. We have never been so busy and yet so malnourished in soul. This is not a technological issue; it is a spiritual emergency.

The Silent Replacement of Spiritual Nourishment

God designed humans to feast on more than bread. In Deuteronomy 8:3, He says, *"Man does not live on bread alone but on every word that comes from the mouth of the Lord."* When this Word is absent from daily life, something deep within begins to starve. Technology has not only replaced books with screens; it has replaced meditation with motion, stillness with scrolling, and worship with Wi-Fi. People now start their days not with prayer, but with newsfeeds. They seek comfort not from Scripture, but from streaming services. Instead of communing with the Spirit, they binge on the digital. This is digital gluttony, a craving that fills the senses while starving the soul.

The Illusion of Connection

Social media promised connection. Instead, it delivered a comparison. People scroll for hours yet feel more isolated, more anxious, and more insecure. They know what celebrities had for breakfast, but have not spoken to their neighbour in weeks. Studies now show that excessive screen time correlates with:

- Depression
- Anxiety
- Sleep disorders
- Decreased empathy
- Stunted attention spans

This is no accident. The system was designed to keep us addicted, distracted, and passive, too occupied to pray, too numb to feel, too tired to resist.

A Biblical Parallel: The Prodigal in the Pigsty

In Luke 15, the prodigal son finds himself far from home, starving not only for food but for dignity and direction. Surrounded by pigs and husks, he comes to his senses. *"How many of my father's hired servants have food to spare, and here*

I am starving to death!" (Luke 15:17). This is the world today feeding on the digital husks of dopamine hits, trivia, and curated illusions, while ignoring the true feast of the Father's table. We are sons and daughters made for spiritual abundance, yet many live like orphans, scrolling in a pigsty.

Fasting from the Digital — A Modern Spiritual Discipline

If processed food destroys the body, then processed content destroys the soul. Just as we detox our bodies, we must also detox our minds. Digital fasting is not about abandoning technology altogether, but about reclaiming boundaries:

- One day a week with no screens
- Mornings that begin in Scripture, not on social media
- Meals without phones, reconnecting face-to-face
- Sabbaths of stillness, silence, and simplicity

Just as Daniel chose vegetables over Babylon's delicacies, today's believer must choose presence over programming. We must feast on truth, not trends.

The Church Must Awaken

Churches cannot compete with Netflix, TikTok, or Instagram by becoming more entertaining. They must become more *authentic.* Worship must become deeper, not louder. Preaching must cut through, not just inspire. Discipleship must be relational, not robotic. God is not calling us to keep up with the digital world. He is calling us to *stand apart* from it. Romans 12:2 reminds us: *"Do not conform to the pattern of this world but be transformed by the renewing of your mind."* That renewal cannot happen while our minds are drowned in distractions.

Feasting on the Word Again

When Jesus said in John 6:35, *"I am the bread of life,"* He was offering more than a metaphor. He was offering Himself as the daily sustenance for weary souls. If we neglect this Bread, we begin to crave lesser things: noise, drama, applause, stimulation. But when we return to Him, we find rest. We find focus. We find peace in the storm of information overload. The world's famine is not only in its food; it is in its faith. We are suffering not only from processed calories, but from processed purpose. Let us return to the table. Not just to eat wisely, but to listen deeply. Let us turn off the screens, open the Scriptures, and remember what it means to truly live. Because man does not live on bread or bandwidth alone.

Chapter 41

The Convenience Trap
How Fast Food Became the New Idol

The modern world runs on speed. Fast cars. Fast internet. Fast decisions. And, most destructively, fast food. What once began as a temporary solution for busy workers has now evolved into a permanent cultural stronghold, an idol that rules breakfast, lunch, and dinner. We no longer eat to live. We live to eat, quickly, cheaply, and thoughtlessly. In this chapter, we examine how convenience has enslaved a generation and become a weapon of global genocide, not through war or bullets, but through cheeseburgers, drive-thrus, and microwave meals.

The Idol of Speed and the Sacrifice of Health

In ancient times, idols demanded sacrifice, livestock, gold, and incense. Today's idol demands no less. The sacrifice is your health, time, and spiritual awareness. People worship convenience by sacrificing:

- Nutritional quality
- Family mealtimes
- Cooking skills
- Personal health
- Cultural food heritage

All in exchange for something fast, cheap, salty, sweet, and available 24/7. Fast food is not just a menu; it is a mentality. It teaches that waiting is weakness, effort is outdated, and the body can be satisfied with imitation.

The Deception of the Drive-Thru Gospel

Fast food chains market themselves like churches:

- Bright signs and logos (icons)
- Comforting slogans ("I'm Lovin' It," "Have It Your Way")
- Emotional experiences tied to food
- Community gathering spaces
- Instant gratification with no commitment

This is the drive-thru gospel, a replacement religion that promises happiness through consumption. And it works. Not because the food is nutritious, but because it is engineered to be addictive.

- High sugar levels hijack the brain's pleasure centres
- Excess salt creates cravings and water retention
- MSG and flavour enhancers stimulate false satisfaction

People return again and again, not because they are full, but because they are never truly fed.

The Economic Oppression of the Poor

Fast food has positioned itself as a saviour to the poor. Cheap meals, dollar menus, combo deals. But behind the affordability lies exploitation:

- Low-quality ingredients sourced from unethical suppliers.
- Communities flooded with fast food but starved of fresh produce.
- Higher rates of obesity, diabetes, and heart disease in low-income areas.
- Economic dependency on industries that profit from disease.

In essence, the poor are being poisoned by affordability. Convenience has become a curse.

Biblical Reflections: Esau's Impulsive Meal

Esau sold his birthright for a single bowl of stew (Genesis 25:29–34). Why? Because he was hungry and impatient. He gave up something eternal for something immediate. This is what fast food culture trains us to do: to trade long-term well-being for short-term comfort. It is not just bad nutrition. It is bad theology. Like Esau, we live in a culture that cannot wait, cannot cook, and cannot discern value beyond the next bite.

The result is a generation that is full in the stomach but empty in the spirit.

The Lost Art of the Table

The early church broke bread together daily (Acts 2:46). Meals were sacred. Time around the table built unity, taught children, and gave room for reflection. Today, meals are often eaten:

- In cars
- In front of screens
- In silence
- In haste

The tray has replaced the table. The slow rhythm of life is set by the ticking of a microwave's timer. We must reclaim the table. Not just as a place to eat, but as a place to gather, pray, heal, and connect.

Practical Exodus: Escaping the Convenience Cult

To defeat the idol of convenience, we must make counter-cultural choices:

1. Cook at home. Teach children where food comes from.
2. Grow what you can. Herbs, vegetables, and even small steps matter.
3. Plan your meals. Preparation prevents desperation.
4. Eat slowly. Chew. Reflect. Give thanks.

5. Keep the Sabbath meal. One meal a week with no rushing, no screens, no shortcuts.

Food must return to its rightful place: not a god, not an enemy, but a gift from God.

Conclusion: From Fast Food to Eternal Food

Jesus said in John 4:34, *"My food is to do the will of Him who sent Me and to finish His work."* His nourishment was not driven by speed or taste, but by purpose. He was full even when His stomach was empty, because His soul was aligned with heaven. This is the invitation to us: to hunger for what matters. To stop bowing to the golden arches and start seeking the eternal table. To choose what nourishes instead of what numbs. Because convenience may save time, but it will cost your life.

Chapter 42

Obesity
The Visible Sign of a Silent War

Across the globe, the waistline has become a battleground. Once considered a symbol of wealth and prosperity, obesity has now become the most visible symptom of a silent war waged not with guns or tanks, but with processed sugars, artificial fats, and addictive food formulas. What we see in the mirror is not just personal struggle; it's evidence of an intentional design to enslave the body and sabotage the soul. This is not merely a health crisis. It is a spiritual crisis.

The Global Expansion of the Obesity Epidemic

According to the World Health Organization, worldwide obesity has nearly tripled since 1975. In 2024:

- Over 1 billion adults are overweight, with more than 650 million classified as obese.
- Childhood obesity is rising faster than adult rates.

- Developing countries are now facing *dual burdens*: malnutrition and obesity coexisting in the same households.

This is not accidental. It is the planned consequence of a global food system that profits from overconsumption.

Designed to Overeat: The Science of Addiction

Processed foods are not just unhealthy, they're engineered to hijack the brain:

- **Hyper palatability:** A formulaic blend of fat, sugar, and salt that bypasses natural satiety signals.
- **Portion distortion:** Larger serving sizes create new baselines for satisfaction.
- **Speed eating:** Soft, pre-chewed textures encourage rapid consumption, leading to calorie overload before the brain can register fullness.

The result? An endless cycle: crave, consume, crash, repeat. The system thrives on obesity. The heavier you get, the more you need medications, surgeries, and special products. This is profitable bondage.

Obesity and the Temple of the Holy Spirit

The Bible teaches that our bodies are temples of the Holy Spirit (1 Corinthians 6:19-20). They are not to be idolised, but neither are they to be neglected or abused. Obesity often arises not from laziness or gluttony, but from misinformation, cultural conditioning, and engineered addiction. But the consequences are still real:

- Cardiovascular disease
- Type 2 diabetes
- Cancer
- Depression
- Infertility
- Lower life expectancy

If our bodies are temples, what condition are we keeping them in? Are they places of life, or monuments to the world's food empire?

The Weight of Shame and Silence in the Church

Too often, the Church has remained silent on this issue. Obesity is rarely addressed in sermons, not because it lacks spiritual implications, but because it touches too close to home. But silence allows suffering to grow. Instead of shame, the Church must offer discipleship: practical help, emotional support, and biblical truth about food, body stewardship, and self-control. Fasting, exercise, accountability, and nutritional education are not just health tools; they are acts of worship.

Jesus and the Multitudes: Feeding, Not Fattening

Jesus fed multitudes with bread and fish, but always in moderation and mindfulness. There were leftovers, yes, but no gluttony. No addiction. No preservatives. Just a simple, divine provision that satisfied both body and soul. Contrast that with today's abundance: excess with no purpose. The problem is not just *what* we eat, but why we eat. Many turn to food:

- For comfort
- For control
- For distraction
- For identity

But only Christ can truly fill those needs. Food cannot save you. Only Jesus can.

Breaking Free from the Weight of the World

To overcome obesity, we must go deeper than diet plans. We need deliverance from the systems that trap us.

1. **Repentance:** not for being overweight, but for trusting in food instead of God.
2. **Renewal of the mind:** transforming our habits and beliefs about the body (Romans 12:2).
3. **Revelation:** understanding the spiritual war being waged through food and rising in wisdom.
4. **Resilience:** embracing small victories, long-term obedience, and grace-fuelled progress.

Conclusion: Glorifying God in Body and Spirit

Obesity is not about vanity. It's about vitality. It's about whether we will be strong enough to run the race set before us, or whether we'll be sidelined by systems that profit from our sickness. God is calling His people to rise, not only in prayer, but in health. Not only in spirit, but in strength. This is not about becoming slim. It is about becoming whole. As Psalm 103:5 says: *"He satisfies your desires with good things so that your youth is renewed like the eagle's."* May we learn to desire good things again, physically, spiritually, and eternally.

Chapter 43
Malnutrition in a World of Plenty

We live in an age where food is everywhere, plastered on billboards, glowing on digital screens, stacked in supermarket aisles, and ordered at the tap of a finger. Yet despite this abundance, malnutrition remains one of the greatest killers of our time. This is the paradox of the modern age: we are overfed but undernourished. It is no longer about how much we eat, but what we eat. Millions suffer from hidden hunger, not due to famine, but due to processed foods stripped of essential nutrients. This is not just poor nutrition; it is planned deficiency, and it's destroying humanity from the inside out.

The Rise of Hidden Hunger

Malnutrition used to mean starvation. Today, it means something far more subtle and sinister:

- **Micronutrient deficiency:** Lacking vitamins and minerals like Vitamin D, iron, iodine, magnesium, and B12, even while eating three meals a day.

- **Empty calories:** Consuming high amounts of sugar, fat, and salt with little or no nutritional value.
- **Stunted growth in children:** Due to low-quality processed snacks displacing real food.
- **Cognitive and emotional issues:** Brain fog, irritability, and fatigue linked to nutrient depletion.

This silent epidemic affects rich and poor alike, and it is being ignored, even as it expands.

The Dead Soil, the Dead Seed, and the Dead Meal

Three key pillars explain this crisis:

1. Dead Soil Industrial farming has depleted the earth of minerals. Crops grown today contain less iron, zinc, and magnesium than they did a century ago. Pesticides and mono-cropping strip the soil of life.
2. Dead Seed Genetically modified organisms (GMOs) are designed for yield, not nutrition. Many hybrid seeds produce visually perfect crops, but are nutritionally bankrupt.
3. Dead Meal: Ultra-processed foods dominate store shelves. These products are engineered to last long and taste good, but they contain preservatives, colorants, and artificial compounds that replace natural ingredients. Even when "fortified," they provide synthetic nutrition, not living food.

The result? A global famine of real nourishment.

The Malnourished Church. This crisis does not end at the dinner table. A malnourished body affects the soul. In the Bible, physical famine often mirrored spiritual famine (Amos 8:11). Today, the Church is often guilty of the same pattern:

- Feeding the people spiritual fast food, entertainment without depth, motivation without doctrine.
- Neglecting holistic discipleship, ignoring the connection between physical health, mental clarity, and spiritual growth.
- Failing to equip families with nutrition, health, and basic wellness stewardship.

Just as processed food weakens the immune system, shallow teaching weakens the Church's spiritual resistance. We need a return to both living food and living faith.

A Biblical Pattern of Real Nourishment

God's original diet for man was found in Eden: plants, fruit, seeds, herbs (Genesis 1:29). These were full of enzymes, fibre, water, and life. They healed the body and supported the mind. Throughout the Bible, God's provision was always real:

- Manna from heaven
- Fresh oil and grain
- Loaves and fish blessed by Jesus
- Water from the rock

God never gave His people synthetic meals. He gave living nourishment that pointed to the true Bread of Life.

Solutions for a Starving World

To reverse modern malnutrition, we must:

1. **Educate:** Teach communities about nutrient-rich foods, natural sources of vitamins, and the dangers of ultra-processed diets.
2. **Reform agriculture:** Promote regenerative farming, organic growing, and soil restoration practices that bring food back to life.
3. **Resurrect traditional meals:** Encourage families to return to home-cooked meals with whole ingredients. Reclaim old recipes and ancestral food wisdom.
4. **Supplement wisely:** In cases of deep deficiency, natural food-based supplements (not synthetic isolates) can help bridge the gap.
5. **Support local growers:** Empower farmers' markets, urban gardens, and indigenous food sources that resist the global food empire.

Conclusion: Feed the Body, Feed the Spirit

In Matthew 4:4, Jesus declared: *"Man shall not live by bread alone, but by every word that proceeds from the mouth of God."* This verse does not dismiss bread; it elevates the need for balance between physical and spiritual nourishment. If we truly believe that the body is the temple of the Holy Spirit, then feeding it with junk is not just unhealthy, it is unholy. This is the time to rise. To plant. To cook. To teach. To bless the next generation with living food and lasting strength.

Because the world is not starving for calories, it is starving for real food.

Chapter 44

The Invisible Menace
Chemicals in Our Food

What we put into our bodies has far-reaching consequences, not just in terms of the calories, vitamins, and minerals we consume, but also in the invisible chemicals lurking in modern foods. Pesticides, preservatives, colorants, flavour enhancers, and hormones have infiltrated the food chain at every level. These substances are designed to make food last longer, look more appealing, and taste better, but at what cost? As we delve into the dangerous effects of these invisible menaces, we begin to realise that the real threat to humanity may not be what we see, but what we cannot see.

The Chemical Revolution in Food

Food has always been subject to natural processes: fermentation, drying, salting, and smoking. But in the mid-20th century, with the rise of industrial farming and mass food production, a new era began, one marked by the widespread use of chemicals.

- **Pesticides and Herbicides:** Chemicals used to protect crops from pests and weeds. However, traces of these chemicals remain on the food we eat, often in dangerous quantities.
- **Preservatives:** Added to prolong shelf life, but often with unintended health effects such as allergic reactions, hormone disruption, and even cancer.
- **Artificial Colorants:** Chemicals that make food look more attractive but have been linked to hyperactivity in children and potential long-term health risks.
- **Flavour Enhancers (like MSG):** Added to enhance taste, but these can overstimulate the brain's taste receptors and lead to addiction-like behaviours.

While these substances may seem harmless in small doses, the problem arises from their cumulative effect. As we consume them daily, over time, they begin to build up in our bodies, leading to chronic health issues that are difficult to trace back to their origin.

The Dangers of Chemical Exposure

One of the most insidious aspects of chemicals in food is that they are invisible. They are not like a visible injury, which we can immediately address. These chemicals accumulate in the body, causing:

- **Endocrine disruption:** Many pesticides and preservatives mimic hormones in the body, leading to reproductive issues, thyroid imbalances, and early puberty in children.

- **Cancer:** Certain chemicals, like artificial colorants and preservatives, have been linked to an increased risk of cancer, especially when consumed over long periods.
- **Neurotoxicity:** Chemicals like heavy metals and synthetic food additives can affect the nervous system, leading to cognitive impairments, mood disorders, and even developmental issues in children.
- **Immune system suppression:** Long-term exposure to food chemicals weakens the immune system, making the body more susceptible to infections and diseases.

The presence of these chemicals has created a health crisis that is not immediately apparent but has devastating long-term consequences.

A Biblical Perspective on Purity

The Bible speaks often about the importance of purity, both in our spiritual lives and in the way we care for our bodies. Leviticus 11 provides instructions about clean and unclean foods, while 1 Corinthians 6:19-20 reminds us that our bodies are temples of the Holy Spirit. We are called to treat our bodies with care, avoiding practices that lead to defilement. If we are to honour God with our bodies, we must reject the modern food system that introduces chemicals designed to corrupt the very health God has given us.

The Hidden Cost of Convenience

In today's world, chemicals are often introduced into food for the sake of convenience. Pre-packaged meals, fast food, and processed snacks are laden with artificial ingredients that are cheap and easy to produce. But this convenience comes at the expense of health, both individual and collective.

- **Cheapness:** Chemical-laden foods are cheaper to produce than organic, natural, or homemade foods.
- **Speed:** Processed foods are designed for quick consumption, making them ideal for busy people who lack time to cook.
- **Shelf life:** Chemicals extend the shelf life of products, meaning food can be stored for long periods without spoiling.

But what is the cost of this convenience? It is life itself, or at least, the quality of life. These chemicals may save time and money in the short term, but they ultimately harm our health in profound ways.

Reclaiming Health Through Whole Foods

If we are to reverse the damage done by food chemicals, we must reclaim health through whole foods:

1. **Eat fresh:** Choose whole fruits, vegetables, and grains that have not been processed or treated with chemicals.
2. **Go organic:** Whenever possible, buy organic foods that are grown without the use of harmful pesticides or herbicides.
3. **Cook at home**: By preparing meals from scratch, you can control the ingredients and avoid hidden chemicals.

4. **Avoid packaged and processed foods:** These are often full of preservatives, colorants, and flavour enhancers that do nothing for your health.

In addition to rejecting these harmful chemicals, we must also educate ourselves about the food system and advocate for cleaner, more sustainable agricultural practices that protect both our bodies and the planet.

Biblical Food Wisdom for Modern Times

Throughout Scripture, we see God's care in providing food that nourishes and sustains. Jesus, the Bread of Life (John 6:35), provides sustenance not just for our souls but for our bodies. The physical and the spiritual are intertwined; our approach to food must honour both. In the Old Testament, the Israelites were commanded to eat certain foods and avoid others, not just for ceremonial reasons but to protect their health. While we are no longer bound by the same dietary laws, the principle remains: God desires for us to be healthy and whole. The choice to eat pure, whole foods is not just a matter of personal preference; it is an act of worship. In caring for our bodies, we honour the Creator who designed them.

Conclusion: Returning to Purity

As we face the unseen consequences of chemical-laden foods, we must return to purity, in what we eat, in how we nourish our bodies, and in how we respect the temple God has entrusted to us.

The battle is not just against hunger; it is against toxicity. It is a war waged in the shadows of the supermarket aisles and the fast-food chains. But through education, intentionality, and a return to biblical food wisdom, we can reclaim our health and turn back the tide of chemical corruption. It is time to restore purity, to eat as God intended, not as man has corrupted.

Chapter 45
The Global Supply Chain of Destruction

In today's interconnected world, food production is no longer a local affair. It is part of a global system that spans continents and is governed by powerful multinational corporations. This vast network of production, transportation, and distribution is often referred to as the global supply chain. However, this chain, while designed to deliver convenience and abundance, is simultaneously contributing to the global destruction of health. The modern supply chain is not just about getting food from farm to table; it is about controlling what we eat, how we eat, and even how we think about food.

The Corporate Monopoly on Food

At the heart of the global food supply chain are a handful of multinational corporations that dominate every aspect of food production, from seed production to retail:

- Seed producers like Monsanto (now Bayer) control the genetic makeup of the world's food supply through genetically modified organisms (GMOs) and patents on seeds.

- Agricultural giants like Cargill and Archer Daniels Midland (ADM) dominate the global grain and livestock industries, controlling the prices and supply of basic foods.
- Food manufacturers such as Nestlé, Coca-Cola, and PepsiCo not only produce processed foods but also exert immense influence over what consumers purchase, how much they pay, and what is available on supermarket shelves.

These companies don't just produce food, they engineer food. They shape agricultural practices, dictate supply chain prices, and use their market power to silence smaller producers and local farmers. In doing so, they often prioritise profit over health and sustainability.

The Dangers of Industrial Agriculture

One of the key factors contributing to the destruction of health through the global food supply chain is industrial agriculture. Unlike traditional farming, which works in harmony with nature, industrial agriculture is focused on maximising yield at the cost of the environment, human health, and biodiversity.

- **Mono-cropping:** Large-scale industrial farms focus on growing just one type of crop, such as corn or soy. This practice depletes the soil of essential nutrients and encourages the use of chemical fertilisers and pesticides.

- **Overuse of antibiotics:** In factory farming, animals are often given antibiotics not just to treat illness but to promote growth. This contributes to the rise of antibiotic-resistant bacteria.
- **Loss of biodiversity:** The global supply chain prioritises crops that are easy to mass-produce and ship, leading to a loss of genetic diversity in food production.

These practices are not only unsustainable but also harmful to human health, contributing to the rise of chronic diseases such as obesity, diabetes, and cancer.

The Environmental Impact

The global supply chain of food is also wreaking havoc on the planet. From deforestation to water pollution, the environmental costs of mass food production are staggering.

- **Deforestation:** To create more space for crops like soy and palm oil or for livestock grazing, forests are being cleared at an alarming rate. This destroys ecosystems, contributes to climate change, and displaces indigenous communities.
- **Water pollution:** The excessive use of chemical fertilisers and pesticides contaminates water supplies, leading to harmful algal blooms, fish kills, and the destruction of aquatic ecosystems.
- **Greenhouse gas emissions:** The transportation of food products across the globe contributes significantly to carbon emissions. Foods that are grown in one part of the

world and shipped to another generate a massive carbon footprint.

These environmental issues are not just abstract concerns; they are directly linked to our health. As ecosystems collapse and resources become scarcer, the impact on human populations will be profound.

Food as a Weapon of Control

Beyond the environmental and health damage, the global food supply chain is increasingly becoming a tool of power. Just as oil has been used as a means of control and manipulation, so too has food.

- **Corporate control:** By controlling the food supply, multinational corporations gain immense political and economic power. They dictate prices, influence policy decisions, and shape consumer behaviour.
- **Debt and dependency:** In many developing countries, farmers are forced into debt traps by corporations that sell them seeds and chemicals on credit. These farmers then become dependent on these companies, unable to break free from the cycle of exploitation.
- **Cultural erosion:** The spread of fast-food chains and processed foods across the world is contributing to the erosion of local food cultures. Traditional diets, which are often more nutrient-dense and sustainable, are being replaced by unhealthy, industrialised foods.

This monopolistic control over food production is part of a broader agenda to control the masses, and it extends far beyond mere economics.

The Response of the Church: A Call for Action

As stewards of God's creation, Christians are called to take an active role in defending the sanctity of life and the planet. The modern food system is an attack on both.

- **Advocacy for fair trade:** Christians must stand up for farmers who are exploited by large corporations, advocating for fair wages, sustainable practices, and support for small-scale, local agriculture.
- **Promote food sovereignty:** This concept emphasises that communities and nations should have the right to control their own food systems, without being dependent on outside corporations.
- **Environmental stewardship:** Christians must promote sustainability, encouraging regenerative farming, eco-friendly practices, and respect for God's creation.
- **Consumer awareness:** We must be informed consumers, seeking out foods that are produced ethically, sustainably, and without harmful chemicals.

The Church must also recognise the spiritual significance of food. Just as the Lord's Supper symbolises our communion with Christ, our food choices should reflect our commitment to honouring God with our bodies and our environment.

A Better Way: Reclaiming the Food System

Despite the dominance of the global supply chain, there are movements rising to reclaim food production and distribution.

1. **Local and sustainable farming:** Many farmers are choosing to grow food in harmony with nature, using organic practices and sustainable methods. These foods are healthier for both the consumer and the planet.
2. **Community-supported agriculture (CSA):** This model allows consumers to directly support local farmers, receiving fresh, seasonal produce in return.
3. **Food cooperatives:** These are community-owned grocery stores that emphasise organic, locally sourced, and ethically produced foods.
4. **Slow food movement:** A global movement that emphasises the importance of eating locally grown, seasonal foods and preserving culinary traditions.

These movements are pushing back against the industrial food system, and Christians should be at the forefront of supporting them.

Conclusion: Restoring God's Design for Food

The global food supply chain has become a system of exploitation of people, animals, and the planet. It is a manifestation of the greed, consumerism, and disregard for God's creation that pervades the modern world. However, there is hope. Through education, action, and advocacy, we can begin to dismantle this system and restore God's design for food. By returning to sustainable, ethical, and nutritious practices, we can reclaim not only our health but also our spiritual integrity. It is time to reject the global supply chain of destruction and embrace the Kingdom economy of creation care, where all people, all animals, and the earth itself are nourished and honoured.

Chapter 46

The Rise of Junk Food and Its Destructive Impact

As we continue to explore the global genocide of the modern age, we must turn our attention to one of the most pervasive and dangerous elements in our food system today: junk food. The rise of fast food, sugary snacks, and ultra-processed convenience foods has become a hallmark of modern society. But while these foods may offer short-term satisfaction, they come at a devastating cost, both to our health and to the well-being of future generations.

The Convenience of Junk Food

Junk food, often defined by its high sugar, high fat, high salt, and low nutritional value, is now a staple in diets around the world. From quick meals to snacks, junk food is marketed as convenient, affordable, and tasty, making it a tempting option for busy individuals and families. Fast food chains and snack manufacturers have capitalised on this demand, creating an industry worth billions of dollars. In many cases, junk food is designed to be highly addictive. The combination of sugar, fat, and salt triggers the brain's pleasure centres, leading to cravings that drive individuals to consume more. These foods are engineered to create a feedback loop of satisfaction and desire, causing consumers to eat beyond what their bodies truly need. However, while junk food may fill the stomach in the moment, it does not nourish the body. It often leads to malnutrition, as essential vitamins and minerals are missing from processed and synthetic ingredients.

The Health Crisis Caused by Junk Food

The consumption of junk food has been linked to a range of serious health conditions, many of which are now considered global epidemics:

- **Obesity:** The rise of junk food has been a key factor in the obesity crisis. Foods high in sugars and fats contribute to weight gain, leading to a host of related health problems such as heart disease, type 2 diabetes, and high blood pressure.
- **Heart Disease:** Diets rich in unhealthy fats and excessive salt increase the risk of cardiovascular diseases. Junk food can lead to high cholesterol levels, clogged arteries, and heart attacks.
- **Type 2 Diabetes:** Excessive sugar intake, particularly from processed foods and sugary drinks, is a major contributor to the development of type 2 diabetes. The body becomes resistant to insulin, leading to dangerous blood sugar levels.
- **Cancer:** Some studies have linked the consumption of certain processed foods and additives to a higher risk of

cancer. For instance, chemicals used in food preservation and artificial colourants have been shown to increase the risk of specific types of cancer.

- **Mental Health:** Emerging research has shown that diets rich in processed and sugary foods can also harm mental health, contributing to mood swings, anxiety, and depression.

The cumulative effect of consuming junk food over a prolonged period is creating a global health crisis, and the younger generation is particularly vulnerable. Children and teenagers, in particular, are exposed to junk food at an earlier age and are more likely to develop lifelong habits of unhealthy eating.

The Corporate Influence and Marketing Tactics

The rise of junk food has not occurred by accident. Powerful food corporations have spent billions of dollars on marketing and advertising, particularly targeting children and low-income communities. They have made junk food a ubiquitous presence in our daily lives, associating it with happiness, success, and convenience.

- **Targeting Children:** Advertisements for sugary cereals, fast food, and candy are often directed at children. These ads use colourful characters, catchy jingles, and fun images to create an emotional connection with young consumers. Research shows that children exposed to these advertisements are more likely to choose junk food and develop unhealthy eating habits.

- **Super-sizing:** Fast food chains often entice customers with larger portions for a small increase in price. This tactic encourages overeating and the consumption of excessive calories, leading to weight gain and poor health.
- **False Health Claims:** Many processed foods are marketed as healthy options, even though they are filled with sugar, artificial additives, and preservatives. Labels like "low-fat," "fat-free," and "gluten-free" are often misleading, masking the true nutritional value of the food.

This marketing manipulation is a deliberate attempt by food corporations to create dependence on their products and to drive sales, regardless of the consequences for public health.

The Spiritual and Ethical Dimensions

As Christians, we are called to be good stewards of the bodies that God has entrusted to us. The Bible speaks frequently about the importance of living in a way that honours God, including how we care for our physical health.

- 1 Corinthians 6:19-20 reminds us that our bodies are temples of the Holy Spirit, and we are to glorify God with our bodies.
- Proverbs 25:27 tells us that "it is not good to eat too much honey," illustrating the importance of moderation in all things.
- Daniel 1:12-15 provides an example of choosing healthy food over what was offered in the king's court. Daniel's commitment to a diet of vegetables and water is a powerful example of spiritual discipline in food.

Junk food, in many ways, violates these biblical principles. It is not about making moral judgments on the occasional indulgence, but about the systematic choice to prioritise health, discipline, and obedience to God's design for our bodies.

The Environmental Cost of Junk Food

In addition to the harm junk food causes to human health, it also has significant environmental consequences. The production of junk food often involves the use of unsustainable agricultural practices, the overuse of resources, and the exploitation of workers.

- **Factory Farming:** The mass production of meat and processed foods often relies on factory farming, where animals are raised in overcrowded conditions and subjected to hormones and antibiotics. This not only affects animal welfare but also leads to environmental degradation, including water pollution and deforestation.
- **Packaging Waste:** Junk food is often sold in single-use plastic packaging, which contributes to the growing global plastic pollution crisis. The environmental cost of this waste is staggering, as plastics pollute our oceans, harm wildlife, and take hundreds of years to decompose.
- **Carbon Footprint:** The global transportation of ingredients and finished products involved in the junk food supply chain generates a significant carbon footprint, contributing to climate change.

Reversing the Junk Food Epidemic

The solution to the junk food crisis requires a multifaceted approach, from both personal and societal perspectives:

1. **Education:** We must educate people, especially children, about the dangers of junk food and the importance of nutritious eating. Parents, schools, and churches can play a significant role in providing the next generation with the knowledge and skills to make healthier food choices.
2. **Healthier Alternatives:** Communities and food producers should promote the availability and affordability of healthier food options, such as fresh fruits and vegetables, whole grains, and lean proteins.
3. **Legislation and Policy:** Governments can regulate food marketing, particularly to children, and encourage food labelling that provides consumers with clear, honest information about what they are eating.
4. **Spiritual Guidance:** The Church must take a stand in promoting biblical health principles, encouraging its members to choose foods that honour God's design for the body and promoting wellness and self-control.

Conclusion: Choosing Life Over Junk

The rise of junk food represents more than just a health issue; it is a spiritual battle that calls for Christians to resist the temptation of the world's empty promises of convenience and instant gratification. We must choose life over junk, both in what we consume and in how we live our lives. As we make these choices, we are not just improving our health; we are honouring God by caring for the bodies He has given us. And in doing so, we become a witness to the world that God's way of living, including His food design, is far superior to the destructive path of the modern food industry. It is time to reject the global epidemic of junk food and embrace a new way of living, one that prioritises health, purity, and the holistic well-being of our bodies, minds, and spirits.

Chapter 47

The Dangers of Artificial Additives in Food

In recent decades, the use of artificial additives in food production has skyrocketed, becoming a hallmark of the modern food industry. These chemicals, which include preservatives, colourants, flavour enhancers, and sweeteners, are designed to extend shelf life, improve taste, and make food visually appealing. However, these additives come with a hidden cost, and their impact on human health is increasingly under scrutiny.

The Rise of Artificial Additives

Artificial additives are now present in nearly every processed food product. From the bright colours of candies to the long shelf lives of packaged snacks, these chemicals have transformed the way food is produced, marketed, and consumed. In many cases, food manufacturers use additives to increase profits by making products more appealing, convenient, and cost-effective.

These additives are particularly common in ultra-processed foods, which make up a significant portion of the modern diet. Some of the most commonly used additives include:

- **Artificial Sweeteners:** Substances like aspartame, sucralose, and saccharin are added to food and beverages as sugar substitutes. They are marketed as healthier alternatives to sugar, but research has raised concerns about their long-term effects on metabolism, weight gain, and gut health.
- **Preservatives:** Chemicals such as sodium benzoate, sulphites, and BHA/BHT are used to extend the shelf life of food products. These preservatives prevent spoilage and reduce the need for refrigeration, but they may also have adverse effects on health, including allergic reactions and cancer risk.
- **Artificial Colours:** Synthetic dyes like Red 40, Yellow 5, and Blue 1 are added to foods to enhance their appearance. While these colours are widely used in processed foods, studies have shown that they may contribute to hyperactivity in children and could be linked to cancer and other health problems.
- **Flavour Enhancers:** Monosodium glutamate (MSG) and other flavour enhancers are used to intensify the taste of food. Although they are generally recognised as safe by regulatory authorities, some individuals may experience adverse reactions such as headaches, sweating, and chest pain.

Health Risks of Artificial Additives

The widespread consumption of foods containing artificial additives has raised significant concerns about their impact on human health. While the full extent of the risks is still being studied, there is mounting evidence suggesting that these chemicals pose several dangers:

1. **Endocrine Disruption:** Some artificial additives, particularly artificial sweeteners and flavour enhancers, have been linked to endocrine disruption. The endocrine system regulates hormones in the body, and interference with this system can lead to a variety of health issues, including obesity, infertility, and metabolic disorders.

2. **Cancer Risk:** Several artificial additives, such as BHA/BHT, sodium nitrite, and artificial colours, have been linked to an increased risk of cancer. Research has suggested that these chemicals may be carcinogenic or may promote the growth of tumours over time. While regulatory bodies like the FDA claim these additives are safe in small amounts, the cumulative effects of long-term consumption are still unknown.

3. **Allergic Reactions:** Many individuals are sensitive to certain artificial additives, particularly preservatives and food colours. These reactions can range from mild symptoms like rashes and itching to more severe reactions like asthma or anaphylaxis. For example, sodium benzoate has been shown to exacerbate asthma symptoms in some individuals.

4. **Gut Health and Microbiome Disruption:** Artificial sweeteners like aspartame and sucralose have been shown to affect the gut microbiome, which is essential for digestion, immunity, and overall health. These

sweeteners may alter the composition of gut bacteria, leading to digestive issues, inflammation, and even insulin resistance.

5. **Neurological Effects:** Some artificial additives, particularly artificial colours and flavour enhancers, have been linked to neurobehavioral effects such as hyperactivity, mood swings, and learning difficulties, especially in children. The controversial link between food additives and attention-deficit hyperactivity disorder (ADHD) is still debated, but some studies suggest a connection.

The Bible's Call for Purity in Food

The Bible offers us valuable insights into how we should approach food, particularly with respect to what we consume and how we care for our bodies. The modern food system, with its reliance on artificial additives, often fails to align with these principles of purity and health.

- Leviticus 11 provides a clear distinction between clean and unclean animals, offering guidance on what should be eaten. While these dietary laws are specific to ancient Israel, they underscore the importance of eating food that is natural, whole, and uncontaminated.
- 1 Corinthians 10:31 teaches that "whether you eat or drink or whatever you do, do it all for the glory of God." This principle calls us to consider the impact of our food choices on our bodies, recognising that what we eat should honour God and promote health and well-being.

- Daniel 1:8-16 recounts how Daniel and his friends chose to eat only vegetables and water rather than partake in the king's rich food, which was likely laden with additives and unclean items. Their decision was an act of faithfulness and self-control, and God honoured their commitment by making them healthier and wiser than the other youths.

The use of artificial additives is a violation of God's design for food. God's intention for us is to eat what is pure, whole, and life-giving. By consuming food that is laden with chemicals and preservatives, we may be compromising the very temple that God has entrusted to us.

The Ethical Dilemma of Artificial Additives

Beyond the health risks, there is an ethical dimension to the widespread use of artificial additives in food. Many food manufacturers prioritise profit over the health of their consumers. The use of cheap, synthetic ingredients allows companies to reduce production costs and maximise sales, often at the expense of quality and human well-being. Furthermore, there is often a lack of transparency regarding the ingredients in food products. Many consumers are unaware of the artificial chemicals they are consuming, as food labels often use vague terms like "natural flavours" or "artificial colourings." This deception not only undermines trust but also exploits the vulnerability of consumers who may not have access to accurate information about the food they are eating.

The Path Forward: Choosing Natural Foods

The solution to the dangers of artificial additives lies in returning to natural, whole foods. This involves making conscious choices to:

1. **Avoid Processed Foods**: opt for fresh fruits, vegetables, grains, and proteins that have not been subjected to artificial additives. Organic produce is often a safer choice, as it is less likely to contain harmful chemicals.
2. **Read Labels Carefully:** Be vigilant in reading food labels and avoid products with long lists of unrecognisable ingredients. Choose foods with simple, recognisable ingredients.
3. **Educate Others:** Spread awareness about the dangers of artificial additives and encourage others to make healthier food choices. The more people understand the risks, the more they can advocate for change in the food industry.
4. **Support Ethical Companies:** Support food manufacturers who prioritise the health of their consumers over profit, and advocate for policies that require more transparency and regulation in the food industry.

By choosing purity, simplicity, and naturalness in our diets, we can begin to reverse the damage caused by artificial additives and reclaim the health that God desires for us.

Conclusion: The Power of Choice

The modern food industry's reliance on artificial additives is a clear example of how far we have strayed from God's design for food. But the power to change lies within our choices. As Christians, we are called to make choices that reflect God's truth and wisdom, including in what we eat. We are not bound by the false promises of convenience and indulgence offered by the world. Instead, we are free to choose foods that honour God, promote health, and nourish our bodies according to His plan. Let us choose the path of purity and wholeness. Let us reject the artificial and embrace the natural, for in doing so, we will honour the Creator who made us and entrusted us with these bodies.

Chapter 48

The Global Food Industry
Profits Over People

The global food industry is a multinational network that connects farmers, processors, distributors, and retailers to create a vast system that feeds billions of people every day. While this system has made food more accessible and affordable, it has also shifted the priorities of food production from quality and nutritional value to profit maximisation and convenience. The consequences of this shift have been profound, and as a result, the health of millions of people worldwide is at risk.

The Power of Corporations

At the heart of the global food industry are powerful multinational corporations that control the majority of the food supply. Companies like Nestlé, PepsiCo, Coca-Cola, and Mondelez dominate the market, producing and distributing a wide range of products that span from snacks and beverages to packaged meals and desserts. These corporations have the power to dictate what is available on supermarket shelves and influence the dietary habits of consumers across the globe. The drive for profit has led these corporations to focus on creating foods that are cheap, mass-produced, and highly processed. Many of these foods are low in nutrients, high in sugar, salt, and trans fats, and they are often laden with artificial additives. While these foods are inexpensive and convenient, they are far from what God intended for us to eat. To increase market share, food companies have resorted to marketing tactics that manipulate consumers, especially children. Bright colours, catchy slogans, and cartoon characters are strategically used to create brand loyalty and encourage excessive consumption of unhealthy foods. The resulting increase in obesity, diabetes, and heart disease is a direct consequence of the food industry's focus on maximising profits, often at the expense of public health.

The Ethics of Food Production

As the global food industry grows, so too does the ethical dilemma that surrounds food production. While the industry has the potential to alleviate hunger and improve living standards, it often falls short in terms of sustainability, fair wages, and environmental responsibility. Industrial agriculture, which is largely driven by the food industry, has contributed to the destruction of ecosystems, the depletion of soil health, and the exacerbation of climate change. In addition, food production has become exploitative, particularly in developing countries. Workers in agricultural fields, factories, and distribution centres often face poor working conditions, low wages, and abuse. Children are sometimes forced to work on farms or in factories instead of going to school. The food industry's insatiable demand for cheap labour fuels these human rights violations, and the result is a global food system that values profits over people.

The Impact on the Poor

The poorest people in the world are often the most vulnerable to the harms caused by the global food industry. While large corporations benefit from economies of scale and cheap labour, the poorest countries and individuals suffer the most. Many low-income communities lack access to nutritious food and are forced to rely on inexpensive, processed foods that offer little in terms of health benefits. This leads to high rates of malnutrition, obesity, and diet-related diseases. For example, in many parts of the world, fast food chains and processed food companies have aggressively marketed their products to low-income communities, contributing to the rise in diet-related illnesses. In some cases, these companies provide financial incentives to local governments to allow their products to be sold, even though they are harmful to public health. Furthermore, the global food industry's reliance on industrial agriculture has created an unsustainable food system that disproportionately impacts the poorest people. Large-scale farming operations often destroy local ecosystems, pollute water sources, and displace small farmers, making it difficult for local communities to grow their food. The result is a vicious cycle of poverty, food insecurity, and environmental degradation.

Biblical Perspectives on Food and Justice

The Bible offers clear guidance on how we should view food and the responsibility we have toward others, particularly the poor and vulnerable. God's heart for justice and compassion is evident in Scripture, and this extends to the way we treat people involved in food production.

- **Proverbs 22:16 warns against exploiting the poor for personal gain:** "Whoever oppresses the poor to increase his wealth, or gives to the rich, will only come to poverty." This speaks directly to how multinational food corporations often exploit workers, paying them low wages while reaping significant profits.
- **Deuteronomy 24:14-15 commands that workers should be treated fairly and justly:** "Do not take advantage of a hired worker who is poor and needy, whether that worker is a fellow Israelite or a foreigner residing in one of your towns." This principle applies not only to agricultural workers in biblical times but also to workers in today's global food system.
- **Leviticus 23:22 shows God's concern for the poor and the marginalised:** "When you reap the harvest of your land, do not reap to the very edges of your field or gather the gleanings of your harvest. Leave them for the poor and the foreigner." This practice, known as gleaning, was designed to provide food for the poor, and it highlights God's heart for generosity and social responsibility.
- **James 5:4 condemns the exploitation of workers, saying:** "Look! The wages you failed to pay the workers who mowed your fields are crying out against you. The cries of the harvesters have reached the ears of the Lord Almighty." This passage underscores the importance of

paying fair wages to workers and ensuring that they are treated with dignity and respect.

The global food industry's exploitation of the poor and the environment contradicts these biblical principles of justice, fairness, and compassion. As Christians, we are called to support food systems that prioritise human dignity, fair wages, and environmental stewardship.

The Role of Consumers: A Call to Action

As consumers, we have a powerful role to play in shaping the global food system. The choices we make at the grocery store, restaurant, and marketplace have a direct impact on the food industry. By choosing to support companies that prioritise ethical practices and sustainable food production, we can begin to challenge the profit-driven motives of the global food industry. Here are some steps we can take as consumers:

1. **Support Ethical Brands:** Choose food companies that are committed to fair labour practices, sustainability, and environmental responsibility. Look for certifications like Fair Trade, Rainforest Alliance, and Non-GMO Project Verified.
2. **Advocate for Fair Wages:** Support organisations and movements that advocate for fair wages and better working conditions for food industry workers.
3. **Choose Local and Organic:** Where possible, buy locally grown food from farmers who use sustainable practices. Organic food is often grown without harmful pesticides and is better for the environment and human health.

4. **Educate Others:** Share information about the injustices within the global food system and encourage others to make more ethical food choices.

Conclusion: A Food System of Justice and Compassion

The global food industry has become a force that prioritises profits over people, contributing to the exploitation of workers, the degradation of the environment, and the widespread health crises affecting millions of people worldwide. As Christians, we are called to seek justice, compassion, and righteousness in every aspect of our lives, including the food we consume. By making more ethical food choices, supporting fair trade, and advocating for justice in the food industry, we can play a part in creating a food system that reflects God's desire for dignity, health, and fairness for all people. It is time to choose a food system that reflects God's heart, a system that promotes holistic health, justice, and compassion for the poor and vulnerable.

Chapter 49

The Destruction of Traditional Diets

Throughout history, human diets have been shaped by the land, culture, and available resources. Traditional diets, often based on locally sourced, whole foods, have provided essential nutrients to communities around the world. However, over the past century, the rise of processed foods, industrial agriculture, and global trade has led to the destruction of traditional diets, particularly in indigenous and rural populations. These changes have had a devastating impact on the health of communities, resulting in the rise of chronic diseases, obesity, and malnutrition. This chapter will explore how the shift from traditional diets to modern, processed food systems has contributed to the global health crisis, and why returning to traditional eating practices can be a key part of reversing the damage.

The Rise of Processed Foods and Globalisation

In the early 20th century, the advent of industrial food production revolutionised the way food was grown, processed, and consumed. The mass production of processed foods, highly refined and often laden with preservatives, artificial flavours, and unhealthy fats, became the norm. Canned goods, snacks, sugary beverages, and frozen meals made their way into homes across the world, offering convenience at the cost of nutritional value. This global shift was driven by the demand for efficiency and profitability. Food manufacturers quickly learned that by using cheap ingredients, artificial additives, and preservatives, they could create mass-produced foods that were inexpensive to produce and had a long shelf life. Unfortunately, the nutritional value of these foods was often stripped away in the process. As industrialised nations began to embrace processed foods, the effects were felt worldwide. Through global trade, these products infiltrated other countries, displacing traditional food systems and practices. In many cases, local farmers and indigenous food producers were unable to compete with the cheap, mass-produced alternatives, leading to the erosion of cultural food heritage and the destruction of local food economies.

The Impact on Health: A Global Crisis

The consequences of this shift to processed foods have been severe, particularly in terms of global health. As countries have become more dependent on industrialised food systems, rates of chronic diseases have skyrocketed. Conditions such as heart disease, type 2 diabetes, hypertension, obesity, and cancer have reached epidemic proportions worldwide. The Western diet, which emphasises high levels of sugar, refined carbohydrates, saturated fats, and processed meats, has been linked to the rise of these diseases. What was once a diet centred around whole grains, vegetables, fruits, and healthy fats has been replaced with an influx of sugary snacks, fast food, and soda. In particular, the dramatic increase in sugar consumption is one of the most concerning aspects of the modern diet. Added sugars, particularly in the form of high-fructose corn syrup, are now found in nearly every processed food, from breakfast cereals to condiments. This excess sugar consumption has contributed to the global obesity epidemic, which in turn has fuelled the rise of diabetes and cardiovascular disease. The destruction of traditional diets has not only led to increased disease burden but has also contributed to malnutrition in many parts of the world. As processed foods have displaced nutrient-dense foods like vegetables, legumes, and whole grains, people are consuming fewer essential vitamins, minerals, and antioxidants, resulting in widespread nutrient deficiencies. This paradox, where people have access to an abundance of food but suffer from malnutrition, is one of the tragic consequences of the modern food system.

The Loss of Cultural Food Heritage

In addition to the health impacts, the destruction of traditional diets has led to the loss of cultural heritage. Food is deeply connected to a community's history, identity, and spiritual practices. For many indigenous communities, traditional foods are not just a source of nutrition; they are also an expression of cultural pride and a means of passing down wisdom and values to future generations. As processed foods have replaced traditional diets, many communities have lost their connection to the land, the agricultural knowledge, and the food traditions that sustained them for centuries. This shift has caused a cultural erosion, where younger generations no longer learn how to grow or prepare traditional foods, leading to the abandonment of important cultural practices and knowledge. For example, in many Native American communities, the introduction of refined foods like white flour, sugary snacks, and soda has resulted in a loss of traditional food practices that once included wild game, fish, corn, beans, and squash. Similarly, in African nations, the rise of processed grains and vegetable oils has led to the decline of traditional diets that included millets, sorghum, and locally grown vegetables. This loss of cultural heritage is not just about food; it is about identity, community, and the wisdom that has been passed down through generations. The disappearance of traditional diets is part of a broader trend of cultural assimilation and globalisation, where local customs and ways of life are replaced by standardised, Westernized practices.

Biblical Reflections on Traditional Eating Practices

The Bible offers valuable insight into the importance of food and diet in human life. God created food not just for survival, but as a means of relationship, sustenance, and honouring Him. The Garden of Eden (Genesis 2:9) provided Adam and Eve with everything they needed to live in harmony with creation and with God. The food given to them was wholesome, natural, and abundant, reflecting God's design for optimal human health and well-being.

- Genesis 1:29 says, "Then God said, 'I give you every seed-bearing plant on the face of the whole earth and every tree that has fruit with seed in it. They will be yours for food.'" This passage highlights God's intent for a diet rich in plant-based foods, fruits, and seeds.
- Leviticus 11 outlines dietary laws that reflect God's concern for both physical health and spiritual purity. These laws were given to the Israelites to set them apart from other nations and to promote physical and spiritual well-being.
- 1 Corinthians 10:31 reminds us, "So whether you eat or drink or whatever you do, do it all for the glory of God." This principle calls us to be mindful of what we consume and how our eating habits reflect our relationship with God.

Returning to traditional diets is not just about improving physical health; it is also about honouring God's design for food and creation. By choosing to embrace wholesome, locally sourced, and natural foods, we align ourselves with the values outlined in Scripture, promoting both personal well-being and cultural integrity.

Restoring Traditional Diets: A Path Forward

While the modern food system has had a profound impact on health and culture, there is hope for restoration. Many communities around the world are beginning to rediscover the value of traditional diets, often with a renewed focus on sustainability and local food systems. This movement is not only about returning to healthy eating habits but also about preserving cultural heritage, protecting the environment, and empowering local economies. To restore traditional diets, individuals and communities can take several steps:

1. **Support Local Food Systems:** Buy food from local farmers, community-supported agriculture (CSA) programs, and farmers' markets that promote traditional farming practices.
2. **Grow Your Own Food:** Start a garden and grow nutrient-dense vegetables, fruits, and herbs to reconnect with the land and reduce reliance on processed foods.
3. **Educate Others:** Share the benefits of traditional eating practices with friends, family, and community members to encourage a return to wholesome, natural foods.
4. **Preserve Cultural Food Traditions:** Learn about traditional cooking methods and recipes from your heritage or other cultures to preserve and pass on the knowledge of preparing healthy, natural meals.

Conclusion: A Return to Wholeness

The destruction of traditional diets has had profound consequences on human health, culture, and the environment. By embracing traditional food systems, we can begin to heal from the damage caused by processed foods and industrial agriculture. The restoration of wholesome, natural foods can lead to better health, stronger communities, and a deeper connection to God's original design for food. As we look to the future, we must recognise the power of food not just to nourish our bodies but to shape our identities, our cultures, and our relationship with the Creator. By returning to traditional eating practices, we can restore the balance that God intended for His creation.

Chapter 50

The Global Economic Impact of Processed Foods

The rise of processed foods has not only had devastating effects on human health and culture, but it has also caused significant disruption in the global economy. The shift from traditional, locally sourced diets to the global industrial food system has created economic inequalities, environmental degradation, and a dependence on unsustainable agricultural practices. This chapter will explore the economic impact of processed foods on both global and local economies, examining how the processed food industry has reshaped supply chains, agriculture, and the labour market.

The Processed Food Industry: A Global Giant

The processed food industry is one of the largest and most profitable sectors of the global economy. According to recent estimates, the global processed food market is worth over $3 trillion annually. This vast industry encompasses a range of products, from canned goods and frozen meals to snack foods, beverages, and sweets. Major companies in this sector, such as Nestlé, PepsiCo, Coca-Cola, and Unilever, dominate the market and have significant influence on food production, distribution, and consumption worldwide. The success of these companies is driven by the ability to mass-produce cheap, shelf-stable food that can be sold at scale across borders. The processed food industry relies on industrial agriculture, which produces enormous quantities of cheap grains, vegetable oils, and sugar, the basic ingredients in many processed foods. In turn, this has led to monopolisation in the global food market, with a handful of corporations controlling much of the world's food supply. The industry's impact on the global economy is profound. On the one hand, the rise of processed food companies has created economic growth in certain sectors, particularly in food production, distribution, and retail. On the other hand, the industry's dominance has contributed to market distortion, the undervaluation of traditional food systems, and economic dependency on unsustainable agricultural practices.

Economic Inequality and Dependency

While the processed food industry has fuelled economic growth, it has also perpetuated economic inequalities. The availability of cheap processed foods has disproportionately benefited wealthier nations, particularly in the Global North. However, in developing countries, the growing reliance on processed foods has contributed to food insecurity and the destruction of local food economies. In many developing nations, the dominance of cheap, imported processed foods has led to the decline of local agriculture and the displacement of smallholder farmers. These farmers often struggle to compete with subsidised, industrially produced foods that are sold at lower prices. This has resulted in the devaluation of traditional food crops and agricultural practices, leading to economic hardship for local farmers and communities. In addition, the global demand for processed foods has driven the expansion of monoculture farming, which is the practice of growing a single crop over large areas of land. Monoculture farming has been linked to soil degradation, loss of biodiversity, and the overuse of chemical fertilisers and pesticides. This not only harms the environment but also threatens the economic livelihoods of small-scale farmers who are forced to abandon traditional, sustainable farming methods in favour of industrial practices.

The Environmental Cost of Processed Foods

The economic impact of processed foods extends beyond the financial realm; it also has significant environmental costs. Industrial agriculture, which provides the raw materials for processed foods, is a leading cause of deforestation, soil erosion, water depletion, and climate change. The demand for cheap grains and vegetable oils has led to the expansion of monoculture plantations, particularly in developing countries. For example, in South America, vast areas of the Amazon rainforest have been cleared to make way for soybean and palm oil plantations, both key ingredients in processed foods. The destruction of these ecosystems not only contributes to biodiversity loss but also accelerates climate change by releasing stored carbon into the atmosphere. Similarly, in Asia and Africa, the demand for sugar and corn has driven the expansion of monoculture farming, depleted the soil, and reduced the land's ability to support diverse crops. Moreover, the industrial farming practices used to produce the ingredients for processed foods are resource-intensive. The overuse of water, chemical fertilisers, and pesticides leads to soil depletion, water pollution, and long-term environmental damage. This not only undermines the sustainability of food systems but also places a heavy burden on the global economy, as countries face the costs of environmental degradation and public health issues related to industrial agriculture.

The Disruption of Local Food Economies

One of the most significant economic impacts of the rise of processed foods has been the disruption of local food economies. In many parts of the world, traditional food systems that were once centred around local farmers, community markets, and family-owned businesses have been replaced by large-scale commercial agriculture and global food chains. This shift has resulted in the consolidation of wealth and power in the hands of a few multinational corporations, while local food producers and small businesses are marginalised. The expansion of supermarket chains and fast-food restaurants has further eroded local food systems, as consumers increasingly turn to inexpensive, mass-produced food options. The disruption of local food economies has had several negative consequences, including:

- **Loss of local jobs:** As small farms and family-owned food businesses are replaced by large industrial operations, millions of workers in the agricultural and food processing industries lose their livelihoods.

- **Loss of food sovereignty:** In many regions, people have become increasingly dependent on imported processed foods, rather than having control over the production of their own food.
- **Cultural erosion:** As traditional food systems are displaced, the cultural practices associated with food production, preparation, and consumption are lost, leading to the erosion of community identities and cultural heritage.

The Cost to the Global Labor Market

The global processed food industry is also responsible for the exploitation of workers, particularly in developing countries. The production of raw materials for processed foods, such as sugar, corn, and vegetable oils, relies on low-wage labour, often in exploitative working conditions. Many workers are subjected to poor wages, unsafe working environments, and a lack of basic rights. In addition, the processed food industry has contributed to the outsourcing of jobs to countries with lower labour standards, leading to the deindustrialisation of certain regions, particularly in the Global North. As jobs are outsourced to lower-cost countries, workers in higher-wage nations face unemployment or job insecurity. This has created a cycle of global economic inequality, where the wealth generated by the processed food industry is concentrated in the hands of a few corporations, while the broader population suffers from economic instability.

Biblical Reflections on Economic Justice

The Bible speaks extensively about economic justice and the need for fair treatment of workers, the poor, and the oppressed. God's Word emphasises the importance of honesty, fair wages, and compassion for those in need:

- **Leviticus 19:13:** "Do not defraud or rob your neighbour. Do not hold back the wages of a hired worker overnight."
- **Deuteronomy 24:14-15:** "Do not take advantage of a hired worker who is poor and needy, whether that worker is a fellow Israelite or a foreigner residing in one of your towns. Pay them their wages each day before sunset, because they are poor and are counting on it."
- **Proverbs 22:16:** "Whoever oppresses the poor to increase his wealth or gives gifts to the rich, both come to poverty."

These passages highlight the need for a just economic system that values the dignity of workers and protects those who are vulnerable. The exploitation of workers in the global processed food industry runs contrary to these biblical principles and calls for a revaluation of how we approach economic relationships and food production.

Conclusion: A Call for Economic Reform

The rise of processed foods has had a profound economic impact on both global and local economies. While it has fuelled the growth of large multinational corporations, it has also contributed to economic inequality, environmental degradation, and the displacement of local food economies. To address these challenges, we must work towards a more just and sustainable food system that values local food production, fair wages, and the preservation of cultural heritage. By supporting sustainable agricultural practices, local food economies, and ethical labour standards, we can begin to restore balance to the global food system and ensure that it works for the benefit of all people, not just a few powerful corporations. This is a crucial step in healing the global economic wounds inflicted by the processed food industry and working toward a future where both people and the planet can thrive.

Chapter 51
The Role of Education in Overcoming Processed Food Dependency

One of the most significant challenges in overcoming the global genocide caused by processed foods is the lack of education surrounding the effects of industrialised food systems on human health, culture, and the environment. In many parts of the world, the rapid rise of processed foods has been accompanied by a decline in knowledge about nutrition, sustainable agriculture, and traditional food systems. This chapter explores the critical role of education in combating processed food dependency and how it can empower individuals, communities, and nations to make more informed, healthier choices about what they eat. The decline of nutritional education for generations, societies around the world had a deep understanding of food and nutrition, rooted in traditional practices passed down through families and communities. However, with the rapid industrialisation of food production, much of this knowledge has been lost. The rise of processed foods, coupled with the decline of home cooking and traditional diets, has led to a knowledge gap about the impact of food on health. In modern education systems, nutritional education is often sidelined or ignored, with little emphasis placed on teaching children and adults the importance of whole, unprocessed foods. Schools tend to focus more on subjects like math, science, and literacy, while food literacy takes a backseat. As a result, people are left vulnerable to marketing campaigns by processed food companies, which use persuasive tactics to make their products seem healthy or harmless. In many countries, children grow up learning little about how food affects their bodies or the environment. Instead, they are taught to rely on fast food chains, snack products, and pre-packaged meals as part of their everyday diet. This has contributed to rising rates of childhood obesity, diabetes, heart disease, and other chronic health conditions that are directly linked to processed food consumption.

The Power of Education to Change Consumer Behaviour

Education plays a pivotal role in reshaping how individuals and communities approach food. By reclaiming knowledge about nutrition, sustainable food practices, and the harmful effects of processed foods, societies can begin to make healthier, more informed decisions about what they eat. The goal is to empower consumers to understand that they have the power to choose foods that are whole, unprocessed, and aligned with biblical principles of nutrition. Efforts to educate the public about the dangers of processed foods and the benefits of whole, natural foods can take many forms, including:

- **School programs:** Schools can introduce nutrition education into their curricula, teaching children the importance of eating whole foods, cooking from scratch, and understanding the links between food and health.
- **Public health campaigns:** Governments and nonprofit organisations can invest in public health campaigns to raise awareness about the dangers of processed foods and promote healthier dietary habits.
- **Community workshops:** Community centres, churches, and local organisations can host workshops on healthy eating, cooking skills, and sustainable food practices. These workshops can teach people how to grow their own food, cook traditional meals, and make better choices at the grocery store.
- **Online resources and social media:** The rise of digital platforms has created new education opportunities. Websites, blogs, and social media channels can be used to share information about healthy food choices, food sovereignty, and nutritional literacy with a global audience.

Reconnecting to Traditional Food Systems

One of the most effective ways to overcome processed food dependency is by reconnecting with traditional food systems. These systems were built on local, seasonal, and whole foods that provided communities with the nutrients they needed to thrive. Traditional diets were often diverse, based on local agriculture, and supported by community-driven practices. For example, in many indigenous cultures, food was seen as a sacred gift and an integral part of community life. Meals were prepared from locally sourced ingredients, and cooking was done with an emphasis on preserving nutrients and flavours. In contrast, the rise of processed foods has disconnected people from the land and from the act of growing, preparing, and sharing food. Reconnecting to these traditional practices can foster a deeper understanding of food and its role in health, spirituality, and community well-being. By reviving traditional food systems, people can:

- **Preserve local food cultures:** Traditional diets are often diverse and rooted in cultural practices that reflect local agriculture and the seasons. Reviving these diets helps preserve cultural heritage and strengthens community identity.
- **Improve health outcomes:** Whole, unprocessed foods are naturally nutrient-dense and can improve health outcomes by reducing the risk of chronic diseases associated with processed foods.
- **Support sustainable agriculture:** Traditional food systems tend to be more environmentally sustainable, relying on diverse, small-scale farming methods rather than monoculture crops that damage the land.

Biblical Principles of Food Education

The Bible provides profound insights into the relationship between food and education. From the beginning of creation, God gave humanity clear instructions about what to eat, and these instructions are rooted in wisdom that promotes health, well-being, and community:

- **Genesis 1:29:** "Then God said, 'I give you every seed-bearing plant on the face of the whole earth and every tree that has fruit with seed in it. They will be yours for food.'" This verse reminds us of God's original design for human nutrition: a diet based on plant-based foods, which are naturally nourishing and life-sustaining.
- **Proverbs 23:1-3:** "When you sit to dine with a ruler, note well what is before you, and put a knife to your throat if you are given to gluttony. Do not crave his delicacies, for that food is deceptive." This passage encourages us to avoid indulgence in excessive eating and warns against the deceptive allure of food that is unhealthy or harmful.
- **Daniel 1:8-16:** In the book of Daniel, we see the importance of self-control concerning food choices. Daniel chose a diet of vegetables and water, rejecting the king's rich food and wine, which was against his principles. His decision to stick with healthy, unprocessed foods led to better health and wisdom. Daniel's example teaches us that adhering to God's guidance on nutrition can lead to both physical and spiritual benefits.

These biblical principles highlight the importance of obedience to God's design for food, which emphasises health, discipline, and self-control.

A Call for Reform in Education Systems

To truly overcome the dependency on processed foods, we must reform the way we educate people about food. We must make nutrition and food education a central part of school curricula and community programs. Governments, schools, and churches can work together to ensure that people of all ages understand the importance of choosing whole, unprocessed foods and the harmful consequences of the processed food industry. By empowering individuals with knowledge about food systems, nutrition, and sustainable agriculture, we can create a global movement toward healthier eating and a more sustainable future. This education is not only a matter of personal well-being but a vital part of fulfilling God's original command to care for the earth and live in harmony with His creation.

Conclusion: A New Generation of Food Educators

The path to overcoming processed food dependency lies in the hands of a new generation of food educators. These individuals will carry the message of healthier eating, sustainable agriculture, and traditional food systems into schools, communities, and homes around the world. As we educate the next generation about the impact of processed foods and the wisdom of God's design for nutrition, we can help restore a healthier, more just food system for the future. Through education, we can reclaim our food culture, heal our bodies, and honour God's creation by choosing foods that nourish us both physically and spiritually.

Chapter 52

Rebuilding the Global Food System
A Call to Action

The devastation caused by processed foods has reached global proportions. From health epidemics to environmental degradation, the consequences of a food system built on industrialised, processed products are undeniable. However, in the face of such destruction, there is hope. Rebuilding the global food system requires a collective effort to shift away from the dominance of processed foods and return to a more holistic, sustainable, and health-centred approach to food production and consumption. This chapter explores the steps necessary to rebuild a global food system that honours God's creation, supports the health of individuals, and nurtures the well-being of future generations.

The Need for a Paradigm Shift

At the heart of the global food crisis lies a paradigm shift in how we view food. For centuries, food was seen as a sacred gift, something to be grown, prepared, and consumed with intention and care. It was a means of nourishing the body, spirit, and community. However, as industrialisation took hold, food production shifted from a deeply personal and community-oriented practice to an industrialised, profit-driven system that prioritised efficiency and convenience over health and sustainability. To rebuild the food system, we must embrace a new paradigm, one that prioritises the principles of stewardship, health, and sustainability. This new food system must be local, organic, and community-based, providing fresh, nutrient-dense foods while minimising harm to the environment and the people who grow it.

A Global Movement for Food Sovereignty

One of the central goals in rebuilding the global food system is food sovereignty, the right of people to control their own food systems. This concept emphasises local control over food production, distribution, and consumption, allowing communities to determine the best ways to grow and consume food in alignment with their needs and values. Food sovereignty is not just about providing enough food; it is about providing the right kinds of food, in ways that are socially just, environmentally sustainable, and economically fair. To achieve food sovereignty, several key actions must be taken:

- **Support small-scale farmers:** Small-scale farmers are often the backbone of food production in many parts of the world. By supporting these farmers through access to land, resources, and market opportunities, we can create more resilient and sustainable food systems that are less dependent on industrial agriculture.

- **Encourage sustainable farming practices:** Regenerative agriculture, which focuses on restoring soil health, increasing biodiversity, and minimising the use of synthetic chemicals, must become the standard in food production. This approach promotes long-term sustainability and addresses the environmental damage caused by conventional industrial farming.
- **Promote food education and awareness:** Educating individuals and communities about the importance of whole foods, seasonal eating, and local food systems is essential. As people learn to appreciate the value of fresh, nutrient-dense foods, they will demand better quality products, shifting the market away from processed foods.
- **Empower communities:** Local communities must be empowered to take control of their own food systems. This includes supporting community gardens, farmers' markets, and cooperatives that prioritise local production and distribution. By strengthening local food systems, communities can become more resilient and less reliant on the global industrial food system.

Reforming the Role of Governments and Corporations

While local movements are essential to rebuilding the global food system, governments and corporations also play a critical role in creating systemic change. Governments must prioritise policies that support sustainable agriculture, protect public health, and ensure food security for all people. At the same time, corporations must be held accountable for the harm caused by their food products. The processed food industry has historically been motivated by profits rather than the health and well-being of consumers. In the pursuit of cheap ingredients and mass production, these companies have often prioritised convenience and cost over nutrition and sustainability. To rebuild the food system, we need:

- **Regulations on harmful additives and ingredients:** Governments should implement stricter regulations on the use of harmful chemicals, preservatives, and artificial ingredients in processed foods. Additionally, there should be clear labelling to inform consumers about the true nutritional value and ingredients of food products.
- **Incentives for sustainable farming:** Governments can incentivise farmers to adopt sustainable farming practices, such as organic farming, agroecology, and regenerative agriculture. This will help restore the balance between human activity and the environment, ensuring that the land remains fertile and productive for future generations.
- **Corporate responsibility:** Corporations in the food industry must be encouraged (and, when necessary, mandated) to adopt sustainable practices and create products that prioritise the health of consumers. This includes reducing the use of additives, preservatives, and artificial flavourings, while focusing on natural, whole food ingredients.

Restoring Health through Biblical Principles

As we seek to rebuild the food system, it is important to align our efforts with biblical principles that emphasise the sanctity of life, health, and creation. The Bible provides timeless wisdom on food and nutrition that can guide our efforts to restore the global food system.

- **Genesis 1:29:** "Then God said, 'I give you every seed-bearing plant on the face of the whole earth and every tree that has fruit with seed in it. They will be yours for food.'" This passage underscores the importance of whole foods and plant-based diets in God's design for human nutrition. The food that God has created for us is pure, unprocessed, and naturally nourishing.
- **1 Corinthians 10:31:** "So whether you eat or drink or whatever you do, do it all for the glory of God." This verse reminds us that eating is not just about satisfying physical hunger, but about honouring God in all that we do. By choosing whole, natural foods, we honour God's creation and acknowledge His provision.
- **Psalm 104:14-15:** "He makes grass grow for the cattle, and plants for people to cultivate, bringing forth food from the earth: wine that gladdens human hearts, oil to make their faces shine, and bread that sustains their hearts." This passage highlights the divine provision of food from the earth and emphasises the connection between health, sustainability, and the natural world. It is a reminder that God has provided us with all we need to thrive, and that we must honour His gifts by choosing foods that promote life and well-being.

A Vision for the Future

Rebuilding the global food system is not an impossible task; it is a journey of transformation. It requires the collective effort of individuals, communities, governments, corporations, and faith leaders to embrace a new vision of food that is health-centred, sustainable, and aligned with God's design. As we take steps toward a healthier food system, we will witness the restoration of human health, the healing of the environment, and the empowerment of local communities. By prioritising whole, unprocessed foods and adopting sustainable farming practices, we can rebuild a food system that nurtures both people and the planet. It is time for us to act. The global food system is at a crossroads, and we can choose a different path, one that leads to health, sustainability, and justice for all.

Chapter 53
A Call to Return to Eden

In the face of the alarming rise of health crises, environmental degradation, and societal breakdown due to the consumption of processed foods, it is time for humanity to return to Eden, to God's original design for what we should eat and how we should live. The Edenic diet was not just about the foods people consumed but about the relationship between God, humankind, and creation. The food that Adam and Eve ate was pure, natural, and directly from the earth. It was a diet of whole foods, reflecting God's intention for health, well-being, and spiritual communion. This chapter explores the biblical significance of God's provision in Eden, what went wrong with the introduction of processed foods, and how we can rediscover the timeless wisdom of God's original dietary instructions in order to heal our bodies, communities, and the planet.

The Biblical Foundation: God's Provision in Eden

When God created the world, He not only created humanity but also gave us a perfect diet from His abundance. In Genesis

1:29, God said: "Then God said, 'I give you every seed-bearing plant on the face of the whole earth and every tree that has fruit with seed in it. They will be yours for food.'" God's provision in Eden was natural, whole, and unprocessed. Every plant and tree He provided was filled with the nutrients necessary for sustaining life. The fruits, seeds, and grains were not only meant to nourish the body but to sustain the soul as well, as humans were to be in relationship with God and with His creation.

The Fall and the Corruption of God's Perfect Design

With the fall of humanity into sin, the perfect harmony between humankind and God's provision was disrupted. Eve's decision to eat from the tree of knowledge of good and evil, and Adam's choice to follow her, led to a shift in humanity's relationship with food and with the world. The consequences of their actions were immediate and far-reaching:

- **Separation from God:** No longer were Adam and Eve in perfect communion with God. This separation also affected their relationship with creation and with the food they ate.
- **The introduction of toil:** God cursed the ground, and from that point on, farming would require toil and sweat (Genesis 3:17-19). This introduced a system of agricultural practices based on hard labour and difficulty, rather than ease and abundance.
- **The corruption of creation:** The perfect, unblemished creation was no longer as it had been. The effects of sin

began to spread throughout the world, influencing how people interacted with food and with the land.

Over time, humanity's quest for self-sufficiency led to industrialisation and the manufacture of processed foods, far removed from God's original design.

The Rise of Processed Foods and the Modern Crisis

As society advanced technologically, the quest for efficiency led to a shift away from whole foods to processed foods. This shift was driven by the desire for convenience, shelf stability, and the mass production of food products. What started as an attempt to simplify food production soon turned into an industry focused on profit at the expense of human health and the environment. The introduction of artificial additives, refined sugars, and preservatives became a norm in the food industry, and the more natural, nutritious foods began to be replaced by synthetic alternatives. Packaged and processed foods, laden with chemicals and devoid of the nutrients God intended, became the cornerstone of modern diets. This shift had devastating consequences:

- **Health crisis:** The obesity epidemic, diabetes, and heart disease have reached unprecedented levels globally. Processed foods have been linked to chronic diseases and nutrient deficiencies that plague modern societies.
- **Environmental degradation:** The industrialisation of food production has caused deforestation, soil depletion, and the pollution of water sources. The use of harmful

pesticides and fertilisers has led to the contamination of the very land that was meant to nourish us.

- **Loss of food sovereignty:** The rise of large-scale agriculture and food corporations has stripped local communities of their ability to control their own food systems. The power to choose healthy, natural foods has been taken out of the hands of individuals and placed in the hands of corporations driven by profit rather than health.

God's Invitation: Returning to Eden

Despite the overwhelming consequences of the fall, God has not left us without hope. Through Christ, we have been redeemed, and He has called us to restore what was lost in Eden. The redemption of food is a key aspect of this restoration. Returning to Eden does not mean we can simply recreate the past, but it involves a return to God's original intentions for food and health. It is a call to reconnect with the land, to cultivate foods that are nourishing, life-giving, and aligned with God's design. This is a process of spiritual healing as much as it is a call for physical healing.

Practical Steps to Returning to Eden

To return to Eden and reclaim God's vision for our diets and health, we must begin by re-educating ourselves about food and its role in our lives. Here are some practical steps that we can take to return to a healthier, more biblical food system:

1. **Embrace whole foods:** Choose fresh fruits, vegetables, whole grains, and healthy fats over processed and refined foods. These foods reflect God's design and are rich in the nutrients that our bodies were created to thrive on.
2. **Support sustainable farming:** Buy locally grown, organic, and regenerative agriculture-produced foods whenever possible. These practices focus on the healing of the land and ensure that future generations will have access to the same abundance that God provided in Eden.
3. **Cultivate food:** Whether through gardening or supporting local farms, we can become active participants in God's plan for food. By engaging in the act of cultivation, we reconnect with the earth and recognise that we are called to be good stewards of God's creation.
4. **Educate others:** Share the biblical principles of food with others. Educate your community about the health benefits of whole, natural foods and the spiritual significance of eating in harmony with God's design.
5. **Pray over your food:** Let us not take our food for granted. Before eating, take a moment to thank God for His provision and ask Him to bless and sanctify the food we are about to eat.

A New Beginning: Restoring Eden on Earth

As we return to the Edenic diet, we are not just restoring physical health, but we are also engaging in the spiritual act of reconciliation with God, with creation, and with each other. When we choose to nourish our bodies with the foods that God designed for us, we are acknowledging that He is the provider and that His creation is good. Restoring the food system is an act of faithfulness and obedience. It is a return to God's original design, where food was not just fuel for the body, but a means of worship, a gift from the Creator, and a source of community. When we eat as God intended, we align ourselves with His purposes and begin the process of healing, not just for ourselves, but for the world.

Conclusion: A New Eden Awaits

In a world that has been ravaged by the harmful effects of processed foods and industrial agriculture, there is still hope. As we return to Eden, we will experience the restoration of our bodies, our communities, and our relationship with God. Through a commitment to whole foods, sustainable agriculture, and biblical principles of health, we can begin the work of healing the food system and the planet itself. God's plan for food was never to harm us but to nourish us. Let us reclaim His original vision, and in doing so, we will experience true healing, a healing that goes beyond the physical and touches the spiritual and eternal aspects of our lives.

Chapter 54

The Role of Faith in Healing the Food System

As we consider the global impact of processed foods on human health, it is important to recognise the significant role that faith plays in the process of healing, not just on a personal level but on a global scale. Healing the food system requires a spiritual awakening to how our food choices reflect our relationship with God, the earth, and one another. In this chapter, we explore how faith can guide us in overcoming the challenges we face in restoring a healthy, just, and sustainable food system.

The Power of Faith in Rebuilding Systems

The Bible is clear that God cares about food, not just as a physical necessity, but as a spiritual practice. From the very beginning of creation, food has been intertwined with God's plan of provision, blessing, and community. Jesus Himself, in His earthly ministry, often used food as a means of teaching, fellowship, and communion. For instance, He miraculously fed the 5,000 (John 6:1-14) and instituted the Lord's Supper to remind us of His sacrifice and provision (Luke 22:19-20).

As followers of Christ, we are called to be good stewards of all that God has given us, our bodies, our communities, and the earth itself. The choices we make regarding food are not just matters of health but are reflections of our faith and obedience to God's principles. This chapter emphasises how our faith in God compels us to be involved in the healing of the food system, not only by making wise personal food choices but by actively participating in efforts to create a food system that aligns with biblical values.

Faith and Food Justice: Restoring God's Vision for Creation

The modern food system is deeply influenced by inequities and injustices that go against God's original plan for creation. The vast majority of industrialised food production is centred on profit rather than people or the planet. Farmworkers are often exploited, and large-scale agricultural practices have caused irreparable harm to the environment. This system also disproportionately affects the poor and marginalised communities, who are often left with limited access to healthy, nutritious foods. In light of these injustices, we must ask: What is our responsibility as Christians in the global food system? How can faith guide us in addressing issues of food justice and equity?

The biblical concept of justice is foundational to understanding the role of faith in healing the food system. God has always been concerned with justice for the oppressed and care for the poor (Isaiah 58:6-7, Proverbs 31:8-9). When we engage in the work of food justice, we are aligning ourselves with God's heart for holistic care, not just for the body but for the community and the environment.

Faith and Sustainable Practices: A Stewardship Mandate

In Genesis, when God created humanity, He gave Adam and Eve a mandate to tend and keep the earth (Genesis 2:15). This mandate is one of stewardship, where humans are entrusted with the care of creation, ensuring that it flourishes and remains sustainable for future generations. Sustainable agriculture is a key aspect of healing the food system. It involves working with the land, not exploiting it; nurturing the soil, not degrading it; and producing food that nourishes both people and the planet. Faith calls us to be responsible stewards of God's creation, and sustainable practices are not just a choice; they are a biblical imperative. This means supporting regenerative agriculture, organic farming, and fair-trade practices that prioritise the health of the earth, respect for workers, and equitable access to healthy foods. By making these choices, we are actively participating in the restoration of the food system, ensuring that it reflects God's original intention for creation to thrive.

Faith and the Global Impact: Mobilising the Church

As we look to restore the food system, the role of the Church cannot be overlooked. The Church has historically been a powerful force in addressing societal issues, and it must take up the call to address the food crises we face today. As believers, we must recognise that our collective faith can bring about significant transformation in the world around us. The Church can be a leader in the movement toward a more just and sustainable food system by:

1. Educating congregations about the importance of healthy eating and sustainable practices.
2. Advocating for policies that promote food justice and sustainability on a local, national, and global level.
3. Supporting food banks, community gardens, and local initiatives that provide access to healthy foods for underserved communities.
4. Engaging in prayer and spiritual reflection on how to address the food system's flaws from a biblical perspective.

By mobilising the collective faith and action of the Church, we can make a profound impact in transforming not only the food system but the very way society views the relationship between food, health, and justice.

Faith, Healing, and Global Cooperation

The global nature of the food crisis calls for cooperation across borders and cultures. It is not enough for individuals or even local communities to make changes in isolation; we must work together as a global body to create a food system that is just, sustainable, and life-giving. Faith calls us to act with compassion for the world's most vulnerable populations, those who suffer the most from hunger, malnutrition, and environmental degradation. As believers, we are called to go beyond our own needs and concerns, reaching out to those who are most affected by the broken food system and empowering them to make healthier food choices.

Conclusion: Faith and the Future of Food

Healing the food system requires more than just a return to natural and healthy eating habits. It requires a deep, transformative shift in how we understand food, justice, and stewardship. Faith must be the foundation of this transformation. As we embrace the call to care for the earth and to nourish others, we participate in the redemption of God's creation and the restoration of His vision for a just and sustainable food system. The future of food is not just about better health; it is about holistic healing for individuals, communities, and the planet. By aligning our food choices with our faith and by advocating for a food system that reflects God's justice and care for creation, we will create a better future for generations to come. This is our divine calling, and it is a call to act with faith, compassion, and responsibility.

Chapter 55

The End Game
Returning to God's Design for Food

As we approach the conclusion of this journey through the global impact of processed foods and their devastating effects on human health and the environment, we must ask: Where do we go from here? What is the end game? How can we return to God's original design for food? This chapter seeks to explore the final steps in the process of healing and restoration: returning to God's design for how we eat, how we live, and how we care for creation. It is a call to return to the foundations of life that God laid out in the Garden of Eden, where food was pure, unprocessed, and in its natural state, intended to sustain, nourish, and bring life.

The Beginning of Restoration: God's Original Plan

In Genesis 1:29, God gave humanity a clear command regarding food: *"And God said, 'Behold, I have given you every plant yielding seed that is on the face of all the earth, and every tree with seed in its fruit. You shall have them for food.'"* This was the original design, food in its purest form, without the contamination of industrialisation, chemicals, or artificial processing. In Eden, God's creation was designed to provide everything that humanity needed to flourish, not just in physical health but in spiritual and relational well-being as well. Food was intended to be a blessing, a way to connect with God's goodness, and a means of fulfilling the command to be fruitful and multiply. In contrast, the modern food system has veered far from this original blueprint. The rise of processed foods has led to the destruction of both human health and the planet's ecosystems. Yet, even during this brokenness, God offers redemption. The path back to God's design for food is not just about avoiding unhealthy foods but about actively choosing the practices and behaviours that align with God's intentions for creation.

Reclaiming the Garden: Steps Toward Restoration

To return to God's design for food requires a shift in perspective, away from consumerism and exploitation toward restoration and stewardship. There are practical steps that individuals, communities, and nations can take to begin the process of returning to a food system that is both life-giving and in harmony with God's creation.

1. Growing Your Own Food

One of the most direct ways to reconnect with God's original design is to grow your own food. This act of gardening is not only an essential skill but a way to restore relationship with the land. Whether through small home gardens, community gardens, or larger-scale agricultural practices, returning to the earth is a powerful way to become more intentional about the quality of food that we consume.

2. Supporting Local, Sustainable Agriculture

Supporting local farmers who practice sustainable and organic farming methods is another crucial step. By choosing to purchase food that is produced with care for the earth, we reject the industrialised, exploitative food systems that dominate the global market. Local, sustainable agriculture reflects the values of community, care, and stewardship, aligning with the biblical mandate to tend and keep the earth.

3. Eating Whole, Unprocessed Foods

The return to God's design also involves a return to whole, unprocessed foods. The biblical diet described in Genesis is plant-based, consisting of fruits, vegetables, grains, and legumes, with an emphasis on quality over quantity. A diet that is seasonal, local, and whole reflects this design.

Processed foods, with their artificial ingredients, preservatives, and additives, distort this divine design. By choosing to eat foods in their natural state, we can begin the process of healing our bodies and minds from the toxic effects of modern eating habits.

4. Practicing Gratitude for Food

In the Garden of Eden, food was a gift to be received with gratitude. In our current food culture, however, we often take food for granted, treating it as a commodity rather than a blessing. Returning to God's design involves reclaiming the sacredness of food, seeing it as a gift that nourishes our bodies, sustains our lives, and fosters our relationship with

God. Through prayer and thanksgiving, we acknowledge that our provision comes from God, and we invite Him to be present in the process of eating. This practice can transform our approach to food and restore it to its proper place in our lives.

5. Advocating for Food Justice

Finally, returning to God's design for food involves advocating for food justice on a larger scale. The broken food system disproportionately impacts the poor and marginalised. To truly heal the food system, we must ensure that everyone has access to the healthy, nutritious foods they need to thrive. This means working for economic equity, environmental sustainability, and ethical food practices.

As Christians, we are called to be advocates for justice, standing with the oppressed and marginalised, and working toward a world where food is not just a privilege but a basic human right. This is a reflection of God's heart for justice and His desire for all people to have access to His abundant provision.

The Promise of Restoration

The journey back to God's design for food is not a simple one. It will require commitment, sacrifice, and collective action. Yet, as we follow this path, we can be assured that God's promises of restoration will be fulfilled. He promises to redeem what has been broken, to heal the land, and to restore His creation to its intended glory. In the book of Revelation, we are given a glimpse of the ultimate restoration when God's

Kingdom is fully realised on earth. The Tree of Life will once again bear fruit for the healing of the nations (Revelation 22:2). This vision is not just symbolic; it is a promise of God's ultimate plan for the restoration of all things, including our relationship with food.

Conclusion: A Call to Action

As we conclude this exploration of the global genocide of the modern age and the role of food in this crisis, we are left with a clear call to action: We must return to God's original design for food, both in our personal lives and as a global community. Through prayer, faith, and action, we can begin the process of healing, restoring our bodies, our communities, and our planet. This is not just a personal journey but a collective mission that requires the active participation of the global Church and all of humanity. The end game is not merely the avoidance of processed foods but the restoration of God's perfect plan for food, one that promotes life, health, and justice. As we take these steps, we participate in the redemption of God's creation and anticipate the ultimate fulfilment of His promise to restore all things.

Chapter 56
The Call to Global Transformation

The destruction caused by processed foods is not a localised issue; it is a global crisis that demands a global response. From the depths of industrial farming to the shelves of grocery stores worldwide, the footprint of processed food is vast, and its consequences are far-reaching. The call for transformation is not just a call for personal change; it is a call to engage in global healing. In this final chapter, we will explore how we, as individuals, communities, and nations, can rise to the challenge of creating a food system that is just, sustainable, and aligned with God's original design. This is a vision of global transformation that requires collective action and the collaboration of faith communities, policymakers, environmentalists, agriculturalists, and everyday citizens.

Global Crisis: A Shared Responsibility

The consequences of the processed food epidemic are felt across the globe. According to the World Health Organization (WHO), diet-related diseases, such as obesity, diabetes, and cardiovascular diseases, have become the leading cause of death in both developed and developing nations. The reach of this crisis is not bound by borders; it touches every nation, every community, and every individual. The globalisation of the food industry has also resulted in the standardisation of diets, whereby processed, chemically laden foods have replaced traditional, natural food sources. As a result, we have seen a decline in local food cultures and agriculture, and an increase in food insecurity and poverty, particularly in low-income countries where access to healthy food options is limited. We must recognise that the problem is systemic. It is not just about individual choices but about the systems that perpetuate these harmful practices. The multinational corporations that dominate the food industry have immense power to shape the global food market. But alongside this challenge lies the opportunity for transformation: by creating alternative systems that prioritise health, sustainability, and justice, we can overcome the global genocide perpetuated by processed foods.

The Role of the Church in Global Transformation

The Church must play a pivotal role in this transformation. Faith communities hold the unique capacity to influence values, mobilise action, and advocate for systemic change. As Christians, we are called to be the salt and light of the world (Matthew 5:13-16), and this includes how we engage with the world's food systems. Through education, prayer, advocacy, and action, the Church can become a powerful force for healing the global food system. Some of the ways the Church can be involved in this transformation include:

1. **Raising Awareness:** Through sermons, workshops, and community outreach, the Church can educate its members about the dangers of processed foods and the importance of eating following God's design. This knowledge empowers individuals to make informed choices for themselves and their families.
2. **Advocating for Policy Change:** The Church has a moral responsibility to advocate for policies that prioritise food justice, environmental sustainability, and human dignity. This includes supporting legislation that regulates harmful food practices, encourages sustainable farming, and ensures access to healthy, affordable food for all.
3. **Supporting Local and Sustainable Initiatives:** The Church can support local, sustainable food initiatives, such as community gardens, farmers' markets, and food cooperatives. These efforts promote local food production and sustainable agricultural practices while providing access to healthier options for communities in need.
4. **Praying for Global Healing:** The power of prayer is immeasurable in times of crisis. The Church can come together to pray for the healing of the global food system, asking for God's guidance and intervention. Prayer is not only an act of intercession but a call to align our hearts with God's will for creation.

The Role of Policy and Global Institutions

While the Church and faith communities have an important role to play, policy and governmental action are crucial in addressing the global food crisis. Global institutions such as the United Nations (UN), World Health Organization (WHO), and World Trade Organization (WTO) must take the lead in establishing global frameworks for food security, nutrition, and sustainability. To foster a truly sustainable food system, governments must:

- Enforce regulations that limit the harmful practices of food corporations, such as the use of artificial additives, preservatives, and genetically modified organisms (GMOs).
- Incentivise sustainable farming practices that prioritise soil health, biodiversity, and ethical treatment of workers
- Ensure equitable access to healthy food by promoting local food sovereignty and reducing reliance on imported processed foods.
- Invest in education and healthcare programs that address diet-related diseases and provide tools for healthy living.

Governments must work together to create a global food policy that respects the dignity of all people and promotes the well-being of the planet.

The Role of Individuals: A Call for Personal Responsibility

While global action is essential, personal responsibility cannot be overlooked. Everyone has the power to contribute to the healing of the global food system through their daily choices. The choices we make at the grocery store, the meals we prepare, and the food we consume all send a powerful message about what we value. Personal responsibility involves:

1. Making informed choices: Educating ourselves about the food industry, its practices, and how it impacts our health, the environment, and the global economy.
2. Supporting ethical companies that produce food in a way that reflects God's design, organic, fair trade, and sustainable practices.
3. Choosing whole, natural foods that nourish the body and honour God's creation.
4. Minimising food waste by purchasing only what is needed and utilising leftovers creatively.
5. Reducing carbon footprints by supporting local and seasonal foods, thereby cutting down on the environmental impact of long-distance food transportation.

By taking personal responsibility for our food choices, we contribute to the global movement toward a more sustainable and just food system.

A Vision for the Future: A Restored Food System

The vision for the future is clear: a food system that is aligned with God's original design, one that nourishes, heals, and restores both people and the planet. This vision is not a utopian dream but a real possibility that requires the collective efforts of individuals, communities, governments, and faith groups around the world. The restoration of the food system will involve a radical shift in how we view food, not as a commodity to be consumed for personal gain, but as a gift to be shared, stewarded, and celebrated. It will require the reclaiming of local food traditions, the rediscovery of healthy eating habits, and the restoration of the relationship between humanity and the earth.

Conclusion: The Global Call for Healing

In the end, the call to action is a call to hope. The global food system can be healed. It is not too late to turn back from the path of destruction and restore what has been lost. By returning to God's design for food, we align ourselves with His redemptive work in the world. As we engage in this global transformation, we must remember that faith is at the heart of the movement. It is through faith in God's provision, His justice, and His love for creation that we will find the strength to persevere. With God's help, we can restore the food system to its intended state, a system that is healthy, just, and in harmony with His perfect design. Let us heed the call to action, embrace the responsibility, and move forward in hope toward a restored food system for the glory of God and the good of humanity.

About the Author

Dr. R. Van Reenen is a distinguished humanitarian, theologian, life coach, and business advisor to prominent mining houses across the African continent. Born in Cape Town, South Africa, he is the eldest son of Bishop Walter James and Maureen Van Reenen and the oldest of five siblings. From humble beginnings and a life marked by poverty, Dr. Van Reenen has journeyed through adversity with unwavering vision and determined focus on his goals.

With a deep conviction to spiritually and economically empower lives, Dr. Van Reenen holds an MBA and a Ph.D. in Religion and Economics. He founded the School of Spiritual Economics, where biblical principles and practical financial wisdom intersect. He also serves as the chairman of Dr. R. Van Reenen Ministries International, a global ministry dedicated to restoring purpose, igniting faith, and advancing the Kingdom of God. In addition, he founded KBFI (Kingdom Bishops Fraternal International), a spiritual alliance that unites apostolic and episcopal leaders across denominations.

Dr. Van Reenen's calling is rooted in his belief that every life has a divine purpose and that pain often serves as a pathway to power. His message embodies perseverance, vision, and faith that refuse to surrender.

Dr. R Van Reenen Ministries
Email: info@drvanreenenministries.co.za
Website: www.drvanreenenministries.co.za

***

www.ingramcontent.com/pod-product-compliance
Lightning Source LLC
Chambersburg PA
CBHW030910090426
42737CB00007B/155